The Western Wadis
of the Theban Necropolis

A re-examination
of the Western Wadis
of the Theban Necropolis

by
the joint-mission
of
The Cambridge Expedition to the Valley of the Kings
and
The New Kingdom Research Foundation
2013-2014

Piers Litherland

The Western Wadis of the Theban Necropolis
First Edition

Published by New Kingdom Research Foundation
54 Eccleston Road, London W13 0RL

Piers Litherland © 2014
Piers Litherland has asserted his moral rights.

All rights reserved. No part of this publication may be reproduced or used by any means without the permission of the publisher.

ISBN 978-0-9930973-0-0

A CIP catalogue record of this book
is available from the British Library.

The author and publisher cannot accept responsibility or liability for information contained herein, this being in some cases difficult to verify and subject to change.

Layout by Kate Buckle

Cover design by Kate Buckle

Printed and bound in Great Britain by
Short Run Press Limited, Exeter

For Mohsen Kamel
in gratitude
for his friendship and guidance

The Western Wadis of the Theban Necropolis

Acknowledgements

We would like to acknowledge the privilege accorded to us by the Supreme Council of Antiquities of the Ministry of Antiquities in being given permission to work in the Western Wadis and the monuments of the Theban Necropolis.

Our thanks to the Minister, His Excellency Dr Ibrahim Ali; to the Permanent Committee of the SCA; to Dr Mohamed Ismail; Mr Abdul Hakim Karar; Dr Mohamed Abdul Aziz; Mr El Qazafi Abd El Rahim El Azab; Mr Ayman Mohamed Ibrahim; Mr Abd El Nasr Hafiz Sinari; Mr Abd El Nasr M Ahmed and our inspectors Mohamed Khalifa and Ms Hanan Hassan Ahmed Hussein.

In addition we would like to thank Dr Ray Johnson, Dr Vincent Razanajao, Dr Fredrik Hagen, Dr Kate Spence, Dr Mansour Boraik, Dr Mark Lehner and the staff of AERA.

The mission would not have possible without the help and good humour of our guards Sheikh Abu El Ez M. Ibrahim, Migahed Khudary Abd El Salam, Sayed El-Tuhamy M. Mustafa, Qenawi M. Saied and Badawi Abu El-Magd; and our driver, El Tayeb Mahmoud Ibrahim Mustafa.

My personal thanks to Geoffrey Martin, Mohsen Kamel, Judith Bunbury, Graham Smith and Stephen Goddard; and, as always, to Johnny Stow, Dick Marshall, David Birt and Jenny Litherland.

Contents

Preface	7
Chapter One - *Background*	10
Chapter Two - *Description*	17
Chapter Three - *Methodology and People*	19
Chapter Four - *Wadi A*	21
Chapter Five - *Wadi C*	34
Chapter Six - *Wadi D*	41
Chapter Seven - *Wadi F*	48
Chapter Eight - *Wadi G*	64
Chapter Nine - *Wadis B & E*	71
Chapter Ten - *Wadi Bariya 1*	73
Chapter Eleven - *Roads and pathways*	83
Chapter Twelve - *Conclusions*	87
Bibliography	90
Picture Credits	94
Index	95

List of Illustrations

Figure 1   Map from Carter's 1917 JEA article.
Figure 2   Carter's sketch map of the Western Wadis in the Griffith Institute.
Figure 3   The Western Wadis today.
Figure 4   The Western Wadis and Wadi Bariya showing mission coverage.
Figure 5   Major roads and pathways.
Figure 6   The routes to Wadi A.
Figure 7   Carter's maps of Wadi A.
Figure 8   Unrecorded graffito in Wadi A.
Figure 9   Top of chamberless shaft.
Figure 10   Top of shaft-tomb 20.
Figure 11   Two tomb graffiti in Wadi A.
Figure 12   Third tomb graffito in Wadi A.
Figure 13   Coptic shelter in Wadi A.
Figure 14   The conglomerate under the cliff-tomb of Hatshepsut.
Figure 15   The conglomerate under the Baraize cliff-tomb.
Figure 16   Satellite photograph of Wadi A.
Figure 17   Wadi A panorama.
Figure 18   Interior of shaft tomb 20.
Figure 19   Approach to Wadi C.
Figure 20   Wadi C cliff-tomb from above.
Figure 21   Carter sketch plan of the Wadi C cliff-tomb.
Figure 22   The Nefrure cartouche.
Figure 23   Wadi C blocking stones.
Figure 24   Blocking stone in the mouth of the Wadi C cliff-tomb.
Figure 25   Wadi C cliff-tomb conglomerate.
Figure 26   Carter sketch plans of Wadi C.
Figure 27   Pit-tombs in Wadi C.
Figure 28   Satellite photograph of Wadi C.
Figure 29   Approach to Wadi D.
Figure 30   Large rock covered in graffiti in Wadi D.
Figure 31   Figurative graffito in Wadi D
Figure 32   Wadi D major features.
Figure 33   Plan of Wadi D.
Figure 34   Wadi D conglomerate.
Figure 35   Wadi D ape burials.
Figure 36   Interior of Wadi D ape burial.
Figure 37   Carter sketch plans of Wadi D.
Figure 38   Major monuments of Wadis C and D.
Figure 39   Approach to Wadi F.
Figure 40   Wadi F topography.
Figure 41   Wadi F topography from south-east.
Figure 42   Ravine in Wadi F.
Figure 43   Bowl and ravine in Wadi F.
Figure 44   Ravine in Wadi F looking south.
Figure 45   Excavations in ravine in Wadi F.
Figure 46   Cascade in Wadi F at northern end of ravine.
Figure 47   Carter's sketch maps of Wadi F.
Figure 48   Carter's sondages.
Figure 49   The pile of "rubbish" Carter thought was tomb chippings.
Figure 50   Amenhotep II graffito.
Figure 51   Side wadi settlement site.
Figure 52   Possible route up through "staircase" to high desert.
Figure 53   Staircase entrance.
Figure 54   Staircase from below.
Figure 55   Routes up to the high desert.
Figure 56   Wadi G.
Figure 57   Wadi G "tongue".
Figure 58   Wadi G Carter sketches.
Figure 59   Wadi G 127 niche.
Figure 60   Shelf in Wadi G 127 niche.
Figure 61   Wadi G 127 niche and pit tomb.
Figure 62   Wadi G 127 niche and conglomerate body.
Figure 63   Wadi G 127 niche tomb sign.
Figure 64   Wadi B looking east.
Figure 65   Wadi B from above.
Figure 66   Wadi B Carter sketch map.
Figure 67   Location of WB1.
Figure 68   Blocking stone in Wadi Bariya.
Figure 69   Hut below rising ground in Wadi Bariya.
Figure 70   Huts below rising ground in Wadi Bariya.
Figure 71   Pottery sherds in WB1.
Figure 72   WB1 shaft tomb site looking south.
Figure 73   Open shaft in WB1.
Figure 74   North end of shaft bottom.
Figure 75   South end of shaft bottom.
Figure 76   North chamber A looking east.
Figure 77   South chamber B.
Figure 78   Room off south chamber B.
Figure 79   South chamber B looking south.
Figure 80   Niched chamber Ba south of south chamber.
Figure 81   Pottery fragments.
Figure 82   WB1 site from south-west.
Figure 83   Sketch plan of shaft-tomb.
Figure 84   Roads and pathways.
Figure 85   High desert road.
Figure 86   Hut on high desert road.
Figure 87   Location of known workmen's huts.

Preface

The survey covered by this report has its origins in work begun in 1998 by the Amarna Royal Tombs Project under the direction of Geoffrey Martin and Nicholas Reeves, in the subsequent re-clearance of the royal tomb of Horemheb (KV57) by Geoffrey Martin between 2005 and 2009 and in my own research into the origins, constituent parts and extent of the XVIIIth dynasty Valley of the Kings carried out in Egypt between 2011 and 2012 and subsequently at Cambridge between 2012 and 2013.

A question which was raised repeatedly throughout these missions was where the royal women and other royal family members of the XVIIIth dynasty were buried originally. Howard Carter had suggested in a 1917 Journal of Egyptian Archaeology article, which took as its focus the cliff tomb and sarcophagus made for Hatshepsut before she became king, that these burials would be found to the west of the main Theban massif in the wadis he designated with the letters A-G. While in Egypt in March, 2012, I began discussions with the Ministry of Antiquities about the possibility of an official expedition to these wadis.

As a result, in late 2012 Geoffrey Martin kindly agreed to lead a mission to re-visit Carter's 1916-1917 coverage with a view to shedding further light on XVIIIth dynasty royal burial activity. In April 2013 we applied for, and subsequently received, permission from the Ministry of Antiquities for the work which is the subject of this report.

Our work continues and it is hoped that this report will be the first in a series.

Piers Litherland
New Kingdom Research Foundation

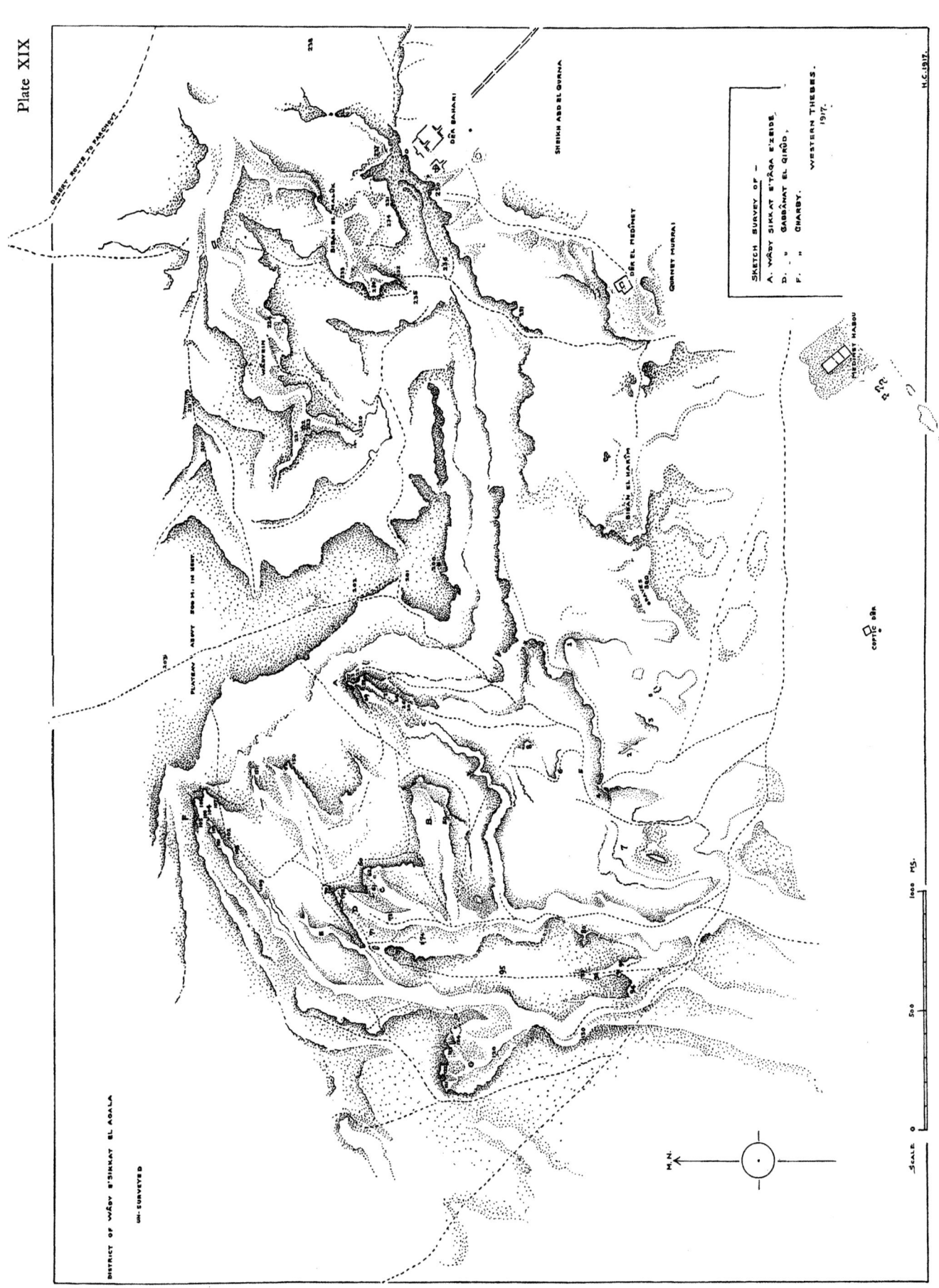

Figure 1. Carter's JEA article map of 1917

Preface

The survey covered by this report has its origins in work begun in 1998 by the Amarna Royal Tombs Project under the direction of Geoffrey Martin and Nicholas Reeves, in the subsequent re-clearance of the royal tomb of Horemheb (KV57) by Geoffrey Martin between 2005 and 2009 and in my own research into the origins, constituent parts and extent of the XVIIIth dynasty Valley of the Kings carried out in Egypt between 2011 and 2012 and subsequently at Cambridge between 2012 and 2013.

A question which was raised repeatedly throughout these missions was where the royal women and other royal family members of the XVIIIth dynasty were buried originally. Howard Carter had suggested in a 1917 Journal of Egyptian Archaeology article, which took as its focus the cliff tomb and sarcophagus made for Hatshepsut before she became king, that these burials would be found to the west of the main Theban massif in the wadis he designated with the letters A-G. While in Egypt in March, 2012, I began discussions with the Ministry of Antiquities about the possibility of an official expedition to these wadis.

As a result, in late 2012 Geoffrey Martin kindly agreed to lead a mission to re-visit Carter's 1916-1917 coverage with a view to shedding further light on XVIIIth dynasty royal burial activity. In April 2013 we applied for, and subsequently received, permission from the Ministry of Antiquities for the work which is the subject of this report.

Our work continues and it is hoped that this report will be the first in a series.

Piers Litherland
New Kingdom Research Foundation

Figure 1. Carter's JEA article map of 1917

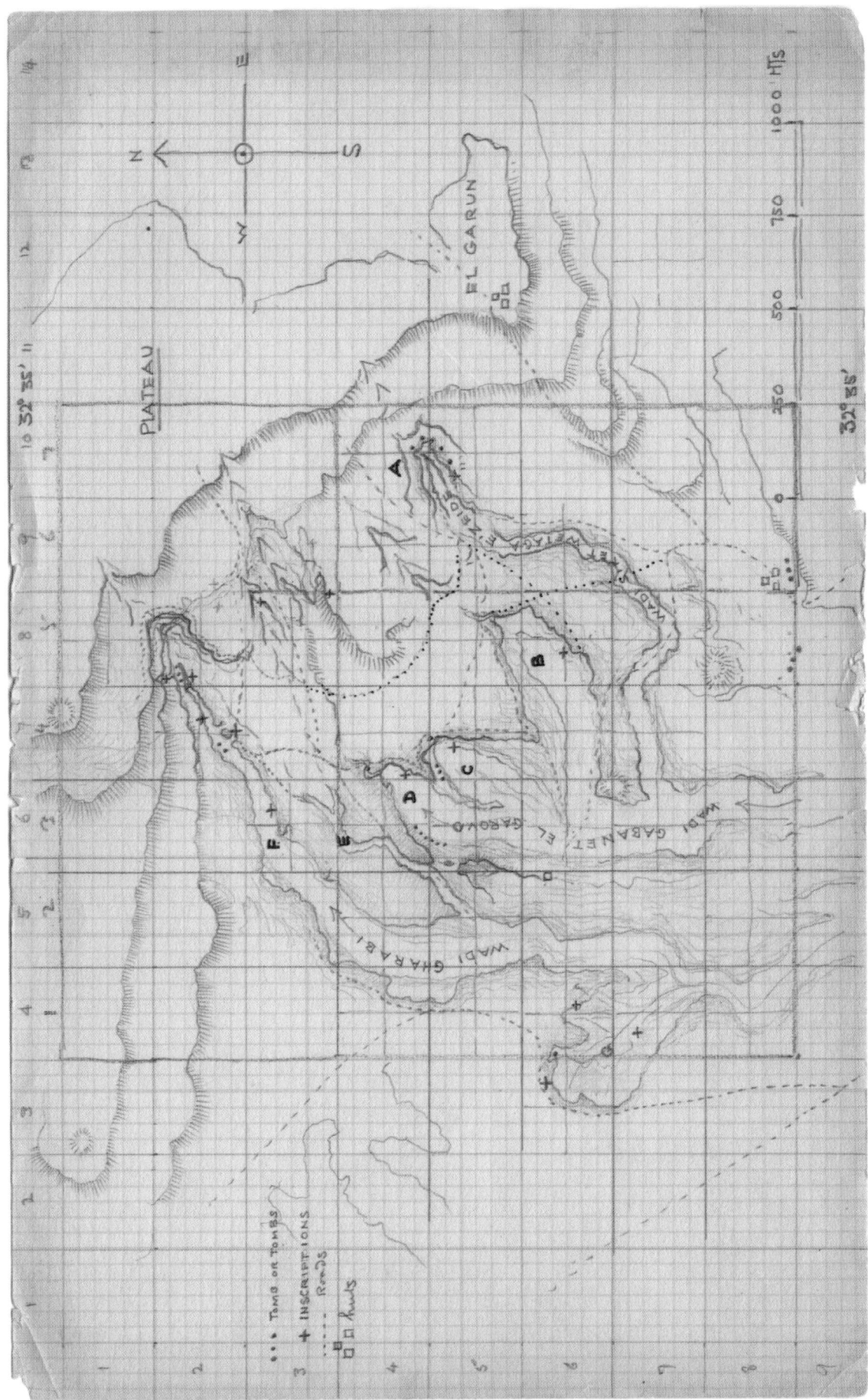

Figure 2. Carter's sketch map in the Griffith Institute. He positions tombs in Wadis F and G not shown on his published map. Note also the blue pencil grid.

THE WESTERN WADIS[1]
CHAPTER ONE - Background

In 1916, as a result of activity following rare rainstorms[2] in the wadis to the west of the main Theban Massif, two tombs came to the notice of local explorers and, subsequently, of Howard Carter who was then working for the Earl of Carnarvon. His resultant inspection of these wadis, which he designated A, B, C, D, E, F and G, produced a map *(Figure 1)* and an article[3] published in the Journal of Egyptian Archaeology, the principal focus of which was the cliff-tomb and sarcophagus prepared for Hatshepsut in Wadi A.

In his article Carter said that he believed that these wadis were part of "the lost cemetery of the royal families". In a sense this burial ground remains lost. The Valley of the Kings contains only two XVIIIth dynasty tombs which can be ascribed with confidence to female royal burials, KV32 (Ti'aa) and KV21 (unknown). Some tombs like WV22 (Amenhotep III) seem to contain suites of rooms designed for royal wives. There are others which were utilised by royal women, like KV60 and the royal cache in the tomb of Amenhotep II (KV35) but these appear not to have been originally designed to contain royal female burials. The University of Basel team excavating KV40 in the Valley of the Kings has discovered a cache of broken objects, some apparently inscribed with the names of royal offspring of the XVIIIth dynasty. Whether their burial here is original or forms part of a re-burial programme is unclear. Situated across the eastern front of the Theban Massif there is a handful of burials, or re-burials, of royal household members. These are insufficient in number to account for all the family members of the XVIIIth dynasty, roughly forty of whom, known by name, are without identified original burials.

In the XIXth dynasty the 'Valley of the Queens'[4] fulfilled the purpose of burial ground for the senior royal family members but there is no equivalent burial ground for the XVIIIth dynasty. Carter's suggestion that the Western Wadis performed this function in the XVIIIth dynasty has never been fully investigated. Some of the wadis have been subject to detailed examination but this western region has never been examined in the light of Carter's central suggestion.

---

[1]The wadis of the title lie due west and, in some cases, slightly to the north of the main Theban Massif. In ancient times the orientation of the Nile was often used to indicate north but with modern maps and satellite photographs oriented to true north, it makes little sense to refer to the site as a whole as "south-western". The site is referred to throughout this publication simply as "the Western Wadis".

[2]James, T. 1992 'Howard Carter: The Path to Tutankhamun', KPI International, London. pp 184-7.

[3]Carter, H. 1917 'A Tomb Prepared for Queen Hatshepsuit and other Recent Discoveries at Thebes', the Journal of Egyptian Archaeology, Volume 4, No 2/3 (April-July, 1917), Egypt Exploration Society, London. pp 107-118.

[4]There was no title 'queen' in ancient Egypt but the name of this location has become embedded.

As a result of the work of Carter, Baraize[5] and, much later, Christine Lilyquist[6], wadis A, C and D *(Figure 3)* have been shown to contain a number of burials. As the XVIIIth dynasty progressed these appear to have moved deeper into the desert and further west.

Wadi A, the easternmost wadi, contains two cliff-tombs, both thought to be of XVIIIth dynasty date. One is anonymous and one was prepared for Hatshepsut and can be dated securely to her lifetime before she made herself king. In Wadi C, further north and slightly further west, there is a single cliff-tomb, ascribed to Hatshepsut's daughter, Nefrure, and thus tentatively dated to the reign of Thutmose II. Further north and slightly further west again, in Wadi D, is the cliff-tomb of the Three Foreign Wives of Thutmose III which dates either to his reign or, just possibly, that of his successor, Amenhotep II.

These wadis have all received published attention, most recently in Christine Lilyquist's superbly detailed publication which concentrates on Wadi D but also covers aspects of Wadis A, B, and C.

Little or no published material relates to the other wadis covered in Carter's 1917 article and the purpose of our mission conducted in 2013 and 2014 was to re-visit these wadis and to re-examine, in particular, wadis F and G and the site in the Wadi Bariya opposite the opening to the Wadi El-Agala also covered by Carter *(Figure 4)*. Carter suggested the latter site dated from the reign of Amenhotep III. If this is the case it would reinforce the idea of the royal burial ground expanding westward and northward away from the main Theban Massif as the XVIIIth dynasty progressed. If activity in Wadis F & G were to date from the period between the reigns of Thutmose III and Amenhotep III then this would clearly be supportive of Carter's solution to the issue of where the missing royal family burials of the XVIIIth dynasty lie.

Some of Carter's notes and sketch maps in the Griffith Institute were used by Elizabeth Thomas in her coverage of these wadis[7]. These maps and sketches appear to show that Carter was aware of more than he published particularly when it came to the suspected locations of new tombs. He produced two reports for Lord Carnarvon on his work in these wadis but these appear to be lost. A photograph album and notebook of Carter's covering the period 1912-1917 which were for sale in New York in the late 1980s have also disappeared.

---

[5]Baraize, E. 1921 'Rapport sur la decouverte d'un tombeau de la XVIIIe dynastie a Sikket Taqet Zayed', Annales du Service des Antiquites d'Egypte 21, ASAE, Cairo. pp183-7.

[6]Lilyquist, C. 2003 'The Tomb of the Three Foreign Wives of Thutmosis III', Metropolitan Museum of Art, New York.

[7]Thomas, E. 1966 'The Royal Necropoleis of Thebes', Princeton.

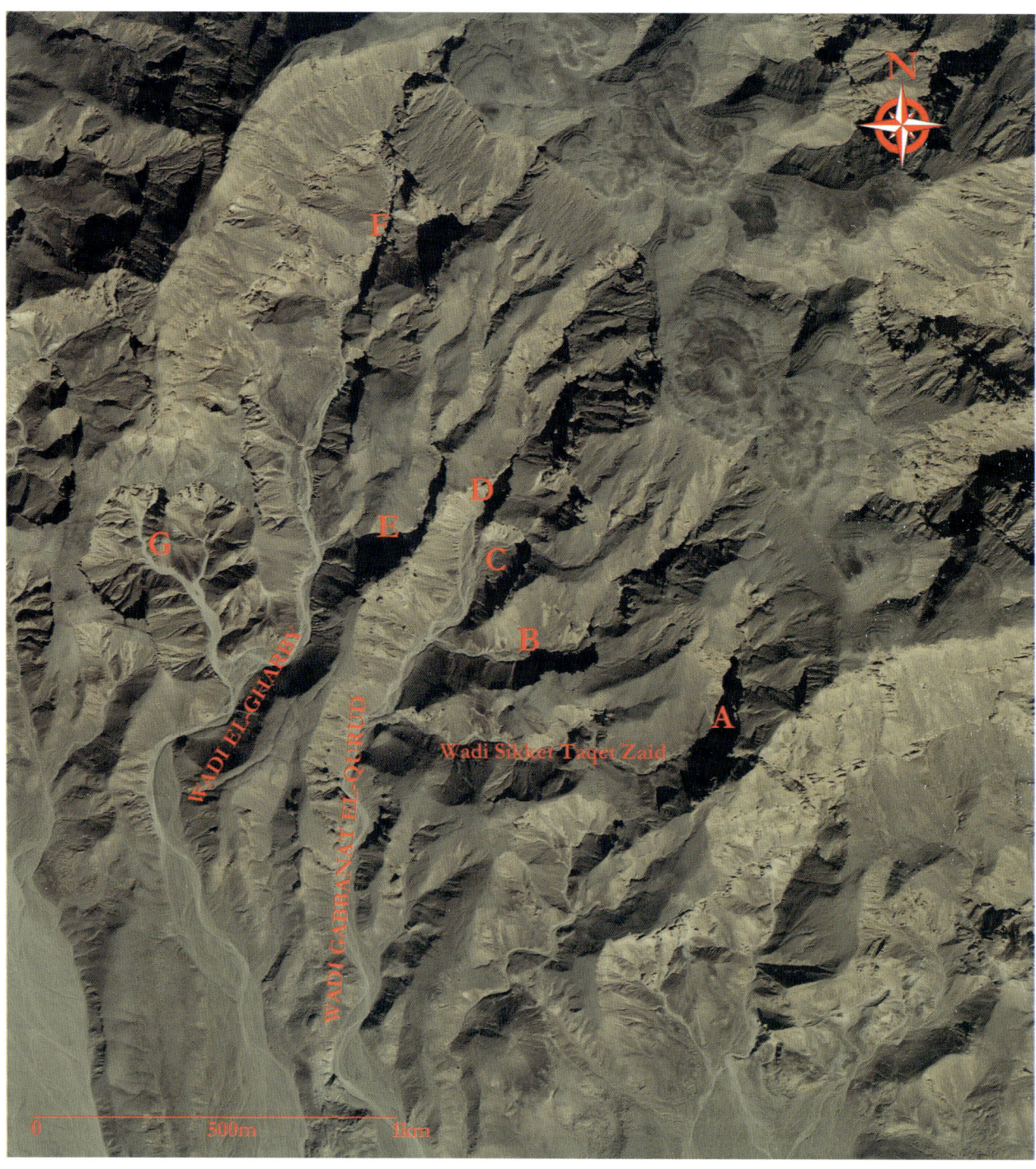

Figure 3. The Western Wadis today

Modern maps of the West Bank tend to stop abruptly with Malqata marking their western margin, the West Valley of the Valley of the Kings their northern margin and Dra Abu el-Naga the eastern extreme. Most of the known monuments are, of course, concentrated within this area. It is possible, though, that thinking about the overall extent of the Theban Necropolis has been limited by assumptions made about the "reach" of the workmen of Deir el-Medina and the ease with which they could be supplied with provisions and, above all, with water.

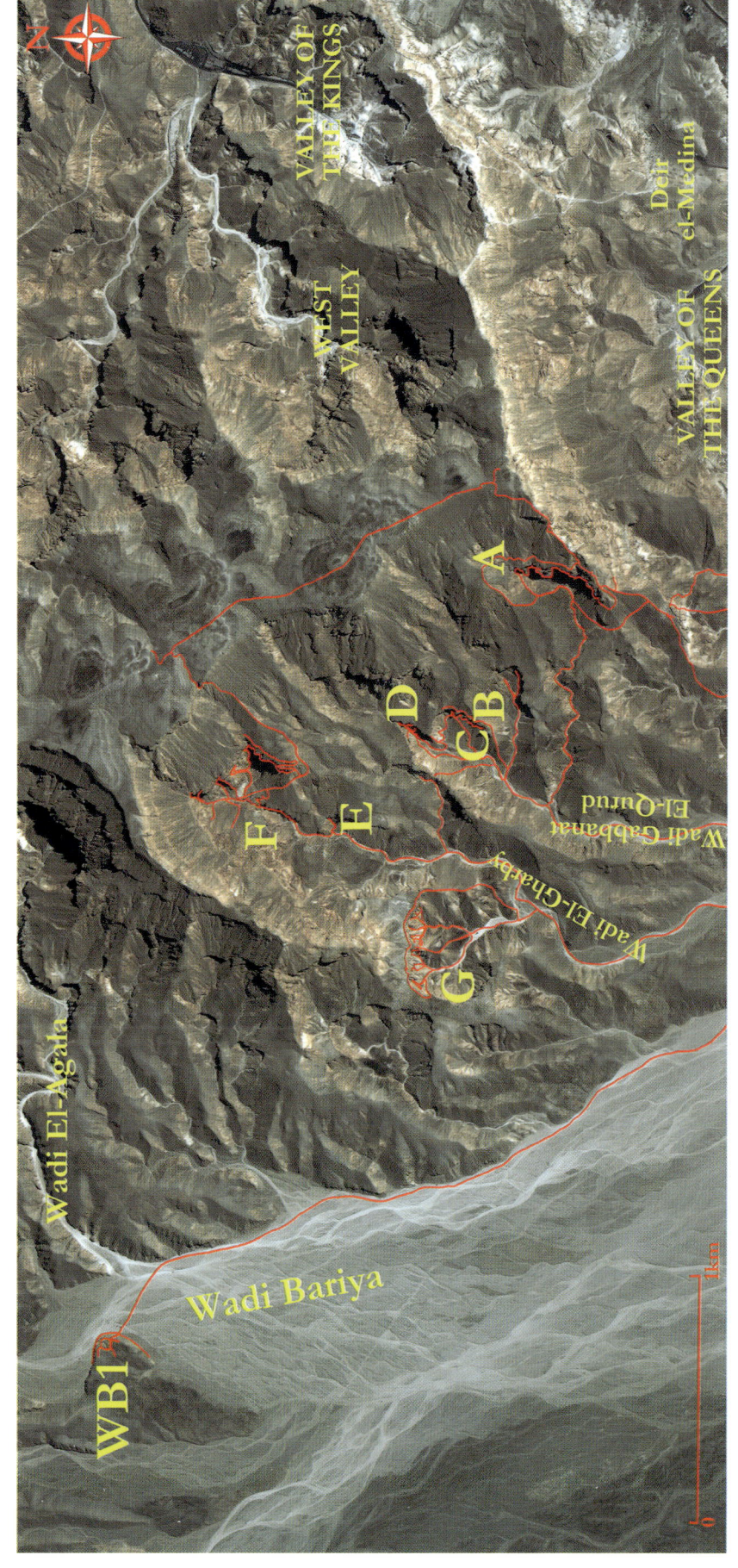

Figure 4. The full area covered by Carter in 1916-17 and re-examined by our mission. Routes covered are marked in red, the main sites are marked in yellow

The Western Wadis of the Theban Necropolis

The Valley of the Kings, the principal focus of these ancient workmen, was within 1.5km of their village. They had to undertake a steep climb up to the saddle on top of the cliffs, and a steep climb down the other side, but a daily commute was not difficult. Similar but marginally longer routes to the West Valley show that all the kings' burial sites were within a three kilometre radius of Deir el-Medina. None was too far from water supplies even if transported readily enough but perhaps laboriously by donkey.

The Workmen's Village at Akhetaten is nearly 7km from the Royal Tomb so perhaps workmen were used to longer commuting distances than we have tended to assume. However, the Western Wadis are more remote still from Deir el-Medina. Activity in these distant wadis demands an expansion in our understanding of the way these workmen operated. The high desert routes to the Western Wadis, partially marked by Carter and visible still (thanks in part to recent use by motorised traffic) on satellite photographs, seem worthy of closer examination as possible alternative access routes to, and indications of, areas of burial activity.

These roads and their tributary paths down into the wadis may be prima facie evidence for burial activity. Many of the paths run along cliff-tops and seem to indicate ancient patrolling activity. Such activity would not have taken place unless there was something to watch over. That something may, of course, merely have been ancient mining (which would be of interest in itself) but it is tempting to believe that there were burials where these paths appear.

If pathways are indicative of policing activity and, in turn, of burial locations, then this has far-reaching consequences for the landscape of the Theban necropolis. Carter's vision of the Western Wadis as the burial ground of the XVIIIth dynasty royal family may be too limited.

From satellite photographs and Google Earth it is possible to pick out a network of paths which connects many cliff-top pathways in large numbers of wadis to the two main high desert ancient roads running approximately from south to north. The easternmost of these heads to Farchout and is joined by its westerly counterpart further north. The eastern road is now obscured by a modern road used by motor vehicles.

This network of paths stretches more than 6km, as the crow flies, to the north of Deir el-Medina *(Figure 5)*. If it indicates activity monitoring burial sites then the size of the Theban necropolis may have been truly vast at some stage in its history - as much as thirty-two square kilometres as opposed to the nine square kilometres currently considered by most Egyptologists.

Figure 5. Some of the major roads (yellow) and paths (red) reaching far to the north and west of the main Theban Massif (the defined ridge in the bottom right of the photograph)

The implications of such a hypothesis, namely that subsequent to the XVIIIth dynasty, when the royal necropolis had increased in size dramatically, a decision was then taken at the start of the new XIXth dynasty to locate burials other than those of the divine pharaohs (which remained in the 'Valley of the Kings') in less remote and ostensibly safer locations, are certainly worthy of examination. This may be one of the factors accounting for the development of the 'Valley of the Queens'. At present the evidence for the dramatic expansion in the Theban necropolis in the XVIIIth dynasty seems to indicate that by and large this development involved provision for the burials of female members of the royal family. A re-examination of the Western Wadis was seen by our mission as a first step in examining these hypotheses.

CHAPTER TWO - Description

The Western Wadis *(Figure 3)* lie between the plain formed by the great Wadi Bariya in the west and the main Theban mountain in the east. Wadis A, B, C, D, E, F and G are all connected to two principal wadis, running roughly north-south: Wadi Gabbanat El-Qurud and Wadi El-Gharby. These two parallel wadis are connected to each other by paths over the dividing ridge.

Wadi Gabbanat El-Qurud

The easternmost of the two principal wadis is the Wadi Gabbanat El-Qurud, which takes its name from the burials of the apes in Wadi D (the terminus of the Wadi). Wadi A is the terminus of a tributary wadi which branches off to the east and is called the Wadi Sikket Taqet Zaid. Wadi A is formed of high cliffs, sitting on a ledge or terrace which then drops further to the wadi floor. The cliffs run only down the eastern side of the wadi.

Further to the north is Wadi B which also opens to the east off the main Wadi Gabbanat El-Qurud. Still further north, as the principal wadi forms its terminus, Wadi C is a bay to the east. The wadi then ends in a sharp V-formation: Wadi D. All three of these wadis. B, C and D are formed by single lines of cliffs which rise vertically from the wadi floor.

Wadi El-Gharby

The westernmost of the principal wadis is the Wadi El-Gharby. This descends in a series of spectacular shelves from the high desert level of 500m above, ending in a ravine, some 20m deep. In prehistoric times this would have drained out into the south-eastern margin of the Wadi Bariya. Carter named his wadis in an anti-clockwise progress from east to west. Travelling north up the Wadi El-Gharby, the first subsidiary wadi encountered is Wadi G which opens to the west off the main wadi. This, like B, C and D is formed by a single line of cliffs which are semi-circular in shape and some 70m in height.

Slightly further north and on the eastern side of the Wadi El-Gharby is Wadi E, a simple bay divided from Wadi D to the east, by a thin spine of cliffs. The Wadi El-Gharby then continues north and eventually narrows into the ravine which forms the lowest level of Wadi F. At its northern end the terrain of the ravine is complicated by large fallen blocks. A dry cascade affords access to a level 20m higher where, again, the bay formed by the cliffs is littered with natural debris, some in the form of smaller water-borne sediments, some in the form of large stones and blocks fallen from the cliffs above.

The cliffs of these wadis provide a large selection of potential locations for burials. Natural fissures, most frequently worn and widened by water flowing off the high desert, were used for the few cliff-tombs discovered so far. Security seems to be the principal reason for choosing these hiding places. The suggestion made that the cleft in the 'Valley of the Queens' might represent the vulva of Hathor[8] could possibly be applied to these clefts, especially as all the known, or intended, occupants seem to have been female. In the absence of textual confirmation this suggestion is perhaps best set aside.

Wadi Bariya

The cliff tombs certainly have a certain 'mystery' about them. The XVIIIth dynasty habit of hiding royal tombs in narrow ravines (KV34), at the bottom of cliffs (KV43, KV38), in water courses (KV20, KV39), under rocks (AN B) encourages the assumption that the tombs of these missing royal family members will be found only in similar hiding places, whether chosen for symbolic or security reasons. The Wadi Bariya site shows that this is an assumption of which to be wary. The lower reaches of the Wadi Bariya consist in a broad, flat flood-plain between 500m and 750m wide. The site we have chosen temporarily to term WB1[9] lies on the far (western) side of this flood-plain on low ground some 15m above the flood plain level. Although the shaft-tombs located here appear to have had no superstructure, the site would have been visible from higher ground on every side. In a sense there was no attempt to mask these burials.

---

[8]LeBlanc, C. 1989 'Ta Set Neferou', Nubar Publishing House, Cairo. p12.

[9]Subject to confirmation by the Supreme Council of Antiquities.

CHAPTER THREE - Methodology and People

Our mission was jointly-led by Professor Geoffrey Martin and myself; we had, in addition: a settlement archaeologist, Mohsen Kamel; two geologists, Dr Judith Bunbury and Dr Graham Smith; and a professional photographer, Stephen Goddard. We were accompanied by two inspectors, Mohamed Khalifa and Hanan Hassan Ahmed Hussein and by up to four guards: Abu El Ez M. Ibrahim, Migahed Khudary Abd El Salam, Sayed El-Tuhamy M. Mustafa, Qenawi M. Saied and Badawi Abu El-Magd. Our driver was El Tayeb Mahmoud Ibrahim Mustafa.

All our work was done on foot and involved walking as many of the routes used in pharaonic times as possible to observe signs of ancient human activity. Our geologists were preparing, simultaneously with our work in the Western Wadis, a report for the SCA on the geology of the Theban Massif.[10] They were therefore able to provide insights into the strata chosen by XVIIIth dynasty tomb-makers, the methods they employed in excavating them and the likely locations of as yet undiscovered burial activity.

We approached the Wadis from the south in a motor vehicle and once further progress became impossible by car, walked, either up through the cliffs south of Wadi A, or through the main wadis (the Wadi Gabbanat El-Qurud, the Wadi El-Gharby and the huge Wadi Bariya) Coverage is shown in Figure 4. Routes which seem entirely sensible in plan, or on aerial views, often prove on site to be very different. It was therefore important to walk as many of the routes as possible. Limited time meant that by no means all the routes of interest could be covered.

All sites and accessible monuments were photographed and, where possible, measurements taken. Graffiti were checked, where previously recorded, and photographed, and new graffiti were numbered and photographed using "Post-it" notes (5cms by 4cms, providing scale) which were removed immediately afterwards so as not to add to the large numbers of pencil and other marks previous missions have left behind.

---

[10] The subject of a separately-published report, Bunbury, J. and Smith, G. 2014 'Valley of the Kings Geological Report', New Kingdom Research Foundation, London.

A number of previously recorded graffiti could not be found in the time available and a surprising number of previously unrecorded graffiti were found. This suggests, perhaps, that numbers left in pencil by Černy and the CEDAE have faded. In some cases, regrettably, modern activity has abraded rock surfaces and modern graffiti have obscured ancient graffiti. The practice of adding notations means that the more obvious graffiti are now surrounded by scratches and pencil marks. In several cases rock surfaces have flaked, fallen or have been eroded since they were last noted. Deciphering these graffiti is one challenge, especially as numbers of them are purely figurative. Ascribing dates to them is a still greater challenge, especially in the more extensively-inscribed wadis where there are large numbers of graffiti.

In the following pages our findings will be presented on a site by site basis, with later comments on the overall landscape and high desert routes and a broader section outlining our conclusions and suggestions for further work. Wadis B and E will be dealt with together out of sequence as neither has produced material of immediate interest.

It is impractical to cover every single graffito examined and so a selection will be covered in the text and a separate publication will be devoted to their overall evaluation.

CHAPTER FOUR - Wadi A

Description

This wadi can be approached from the south by two different routes. It can be reached via the Wadi Gabbanat El-Qurud along the thin, winding side wadi known as the Wadi Sikket Taqet Zaid. Alternatively, it can be approached by a more direct, but steeper, route which cuts up through a staircase in the cliffs, passes through a substantial ancient settlement site and then descends into Wadi A *(Figure 6)*.

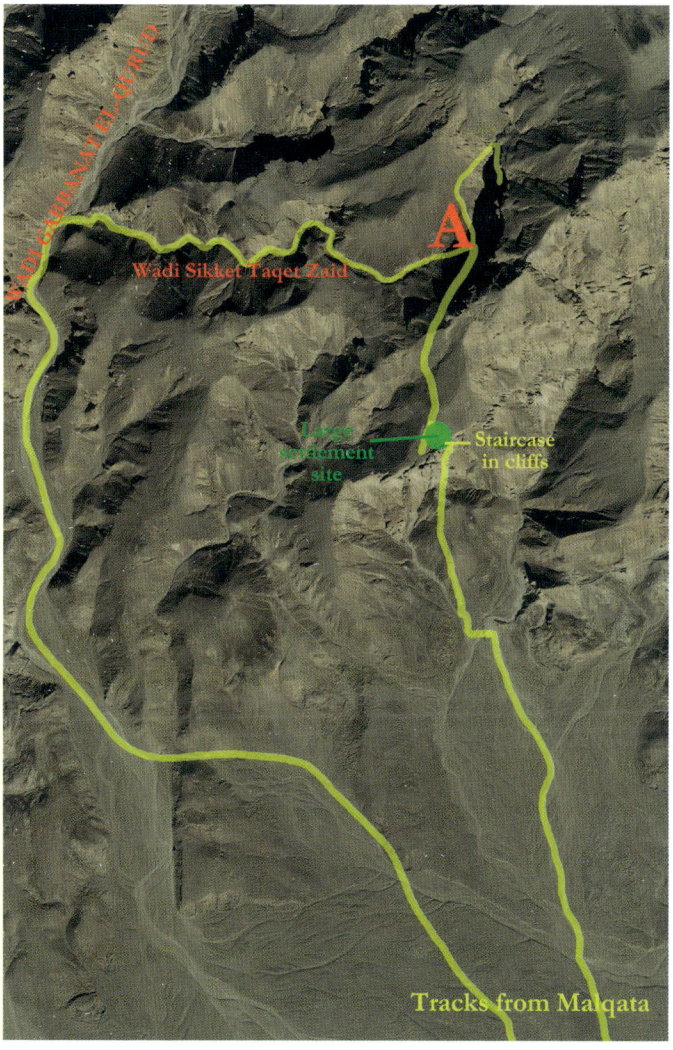

Figure 6. The routes to Wadi A.

Wadi A forms the terminus and northern end of the Wadi Sikket Taqet Zaid *(Figure 6)*. The cliff-tops which line the eastern side of the wadi are some 100m to 120m above the wadi floor and 70m above a ledge, or terrace, which follows the line of the cliffs. The western side of the wadi is largely open with a rising slope which meets the cliffs at the northern end.

The path originally built by Baraize (which approaches the shelf below Hatshepsut's tomb from the western side of the wadi, climbing to shelf level and then turning back down the eastern side of the wadi) has been much-used in the last decade. Modern visitors have scratched graffiti on the cliff-walls and have also drawn with blue paint and charcoal.

There is excavation debris spilling from the mouths of the two shafts at the foot of the cliffs at terrace level and sherds are discernible amongst this debris. It is not clear whether this debris relates to the investigations of Carter and Baraize or if it is of more recent date.

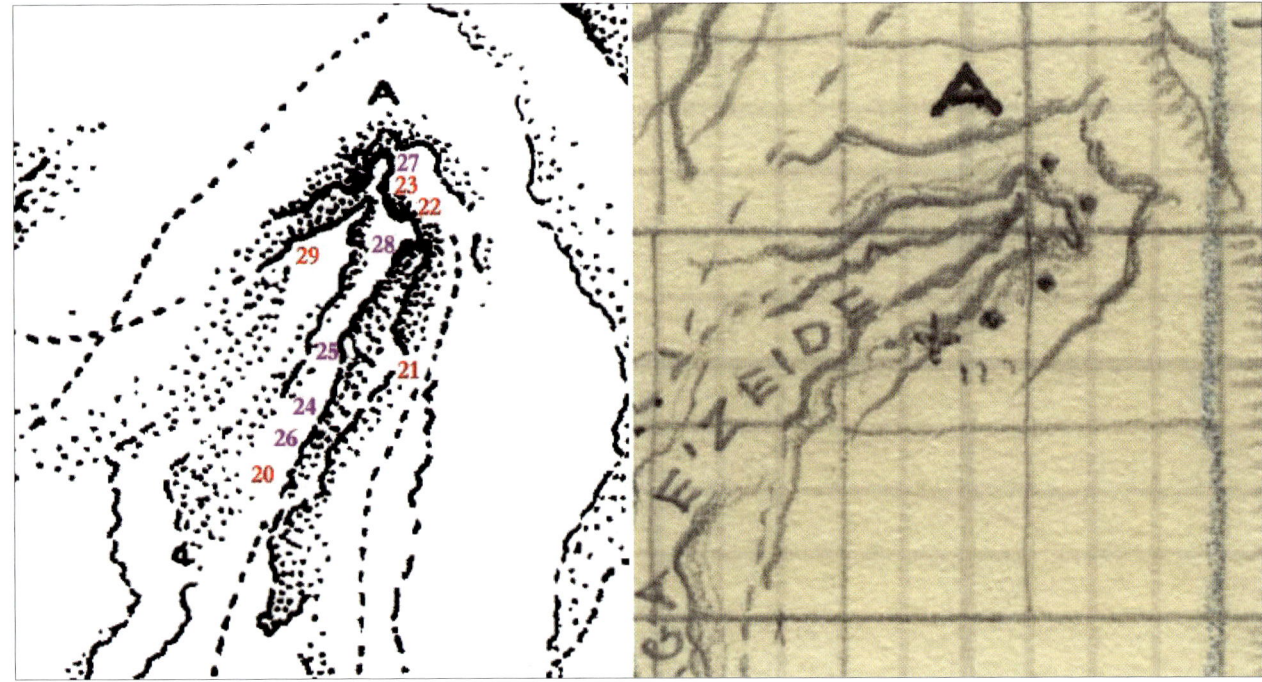

Figure 7. Carter's maps of Wadi A.

Carter's maps of this wadi *(Figure 7)* are slightly confusing, not least because they show the wadi bending to the west. He identified two shaft tombs, (20 and 23), a Coptic shelter (29) and two cliff tombs (22 and 21). Numbers 24-28 are graffiti locations. The precise positions he indicates with his numbers are less clear than they might be. In the case of the two cliff tombs this is not a problem. However he shows a northern shaft tomb which is either now buried under rubble or is shown in the wrong place. There is in fact only one shaft-tomb visible in the wadi (numbered 20 on Carter's map). The other visible shaft is simply that, a shaft which has no discernible chamber at the bottom. It may be that the bottom of the shaft is still blocked with very hard debris concealing a deeper shaft but the bottom appeared solid when the shaft was entered.

Elizabeth Thomas refers to "two queens' tombs and three pits" on the assumption that Carter's third tomb (which she calls Tomb E)[11] is buried. We could find no trace of this third tomb but there is a previously unrecorded graffito above the most likely location *(Figure 8)*.

[11]Thomas, E. op. cit. p196.

Carter produced a plan and section of Hatshepsut's cliff-tomb. He regarded the tomb as being unfinished. Baraize later produced a plan and section of both the Hatshepsut cliff-tomb (which he believed, contra Carter, was complete) and the tomb which bears his name. The latter was apparently sealed but Thomas believed it must have been robbed in antiquity[12].

Figure 8. Unrecorded cross-hatched graffito above possible position of Carter's 23. The photograph has been digitally enhanced to highlight the graffito in red.

An important feature of this wadi is that neither of the cliff-tombs is visible when approached from the south. The Baraize tomb remains hidden at all times behind a vertical ridge of rock and it is astonishing that its location was ever discovered. The tomb built for Hatshepsut is hidden by a large buttress of rock and it is not until seen from below that its position becomes obvious. However, in contrast to the Baraize tomb, once the cleft is in view the opening to the tomb is visible and would have been in ancient times from the slope opposite, even if sealed and plastered.

Both these tombs are some 30m above the rock shelf and how they were cut and how, in particular, it was possible to introduce a heavy stone sarcophagus and lid into the Hatshepsut cliff-tomb has long been a puzzle.

Graffiti

Černy recorded seven graffiti on the terrace or shelf above the shafts and below the cliff-tombs in Wadi A. The name of the XXIst dynasty scribe Butehamun appears in two locations apparently connected with the shaft and shaft-tomb. Above the shaft-tomb (20) Butehamun's name appears on its own, twice. Beside the shaft, below and to the south of the Baraize cliff-tomb, Butehamun's name again appears twice, as does the name Nainudjem[13].

---

[12]Thomas, E. op. cit. p194 and Baraize, E. op. cit p183.

[13]Nainudjem or Nau-nedjem bore the title 'Servant in the Place of Truth'. See Rzepka, S. 2000 "Rock graffiti above the temple of Hatshepsut", Polish Archaeology in the Mediterranean XI, Warsaw.

Carter noted the name Amen(neb)nesttawynakhte to the north of shaft 21. Below the cliff-tomb of Hatshepsut he also noted three petroglyphs which take the form of signs which have been interpreted as 'tomb' signs *(Figures 11 and 12)*. Two of these signs are side-by-side and a third 45cms away to the left. The cliff walls in this bay beneath the cliff-tomb have been particularly heavily defaced.

There are other graffiti along this shelf level apparently unconnected with tomb positions, between the two cliff-tombs *(Figure 17)*. Here, where the path between the two reaches a high point, the names Ity and Amenhotep were noted by Carter.

Most of the graffiti in this wadi are close to the more obvious evidence of tombs. Signs of work on the natural clefts into which the shaft and shaft-tomb (20) have been sunk would quite likely have been evident to inspectors working along the shelf at the foot of the cliffs *(Figures 9 and 10)*.

Figure 9. The shaft with no chamber at the bottom. The working in the rock would have been visible to anyone inspecting the wadi even when the shaft itself was buried.

The Western Wadis of the Theban Necropolis

Figure 10. Carter's shaft-tomb 20. Again the working of this natural fissure would have been visible even when the shaft was buried.

*Figure 11. Two 'tomb' graffiti on rock to south-west of Hatshepsut's cliff tomb.
The photograph has been digitally enhanced to show the signs highlighted in red.*

*Figure 12. Third 'tomb' graffito just below the two in Figure 11.
the photograph has been digitally enhanced to show the sign highlighted in red.*

Butehamun is known to have worked during the late XXth and XXIst dynasties, under the high-priest and general Herihor, under Smendes, Pinudjem I and Pinudjem II, to clear and re-organise the royal burials[14]. His name, those of his father and sons and other apparently contemporary inhabitants of the Deir El-Medina Workmen's Village appear all over the Theban necropolis and it seems reasonable to relate their presence in this wadi to the inspection and clearance of burials[15].

Below the cliff-tomb prepared for Hatshepsut and on the opposite side of the wadi near the wadi floor is a rock-cut shelter which Carter identified as being Coptic *(Figure 11)*. This shelter is open to the elements and has not been the subject of further study.

Observations

Carter believed that this wadi might contain additional burials. Unofficial and illicit attention to these wadis appears to have been fairly constant and many visitors of all sorts have picked over these cliffs. It would be surprising if there were additional burials here but the Baraize tomb demonstrates how well-hidden these can be.

---

[14] Reeves, C.N. 1990 'Valley of the Kings', KPI, London. pp244-5.

[15] Reeves, C.N. op. cit. and Černy, J. 2001 'A Community of Workmen at Thebes in the Ramesside Period', IFAO, Cairo.

Figure 13. Coptic shelter noted by Carter.

It is a feature of many of the Western Wadis that over a long period of time waterborne debris has accumulated at the base of the cliffs below the gullies and gorges through which water has flowed. This debris forms a fan-like ramp of hard but ultimately friable conglomerate *(Figures 14 and 15)*. Judith Bunbury was the first to note that such accumulations of conglomerate had previously been in place under the cliff-tombs in Wadi A.

These accumulations of natural debris would have made the clefts into which the tombs were cut very much easier to reach and would, of course, have provided a natural ramp which would have assisted in the insertion of the sarcophagus. That these ramps were subsequently cut away is clear from the survival of parts of the conglomerate body, usually to one side (in the case of both cliff-tombs in Wadi A, to the left when facing the cliff).

Once the conglomerate was cut away after the tomb was completed, the exposed cliff-face immediately under the tomb entrance was further cut back to impede access. It may be that such artificial cutting-back of the cliff face was a tell-tale sign read by Butehamun and his scribes. However, given the survival intact into modern times of at least one cliff-tomb (in Wadi D) this is open to question.

Figure 14. Conjectural shape of conglomerate accumulation beneath Hatshepsut's cliff-tomb.

Figure 13. Coptic shelter noted by Carter.

It is a feature of many of the Western Wadis that over a long period of time waterborne debris has accumulated at the base of the cliffs below the gullies and gorges through which water has flowed. This debris forms a fan-like ramp of hard but ultimately friable conglomerate *(Figures 14 and 15)*. Judith Bunbury was the first to note that such accumulations of conglomerate had previously been in place under the cliff-tombs in Wadi A.

These accumulations of natural debris would have made the clefts into which the tombs were cut very much easier to reach and would, of course, have provided a natural ramp which would have assisted in the insertion of the sarcophagus. That these ramps were subsequently cut away is clear from the survival of parts of the conglomerate body, usually to one side (in the case of both cliff-tombs in Wadi A, to the left when facing the cliff).

Once the conglomerate was cut away after the tomb was completed, the exposed cliff-face immediately under the tomb entrance was further cut back to impede access. It may be that such artificial cutting-back of the cliff face was a tell-tale sign read by Butehamun and his scribes. However, given the survival intact into modern times of at least one cliff-tomb (in Wadi D) this is open to question.

Figure 14. Conjectural shape of conglomerate accumulation beneath Hatshepsut's cliff-tomb.

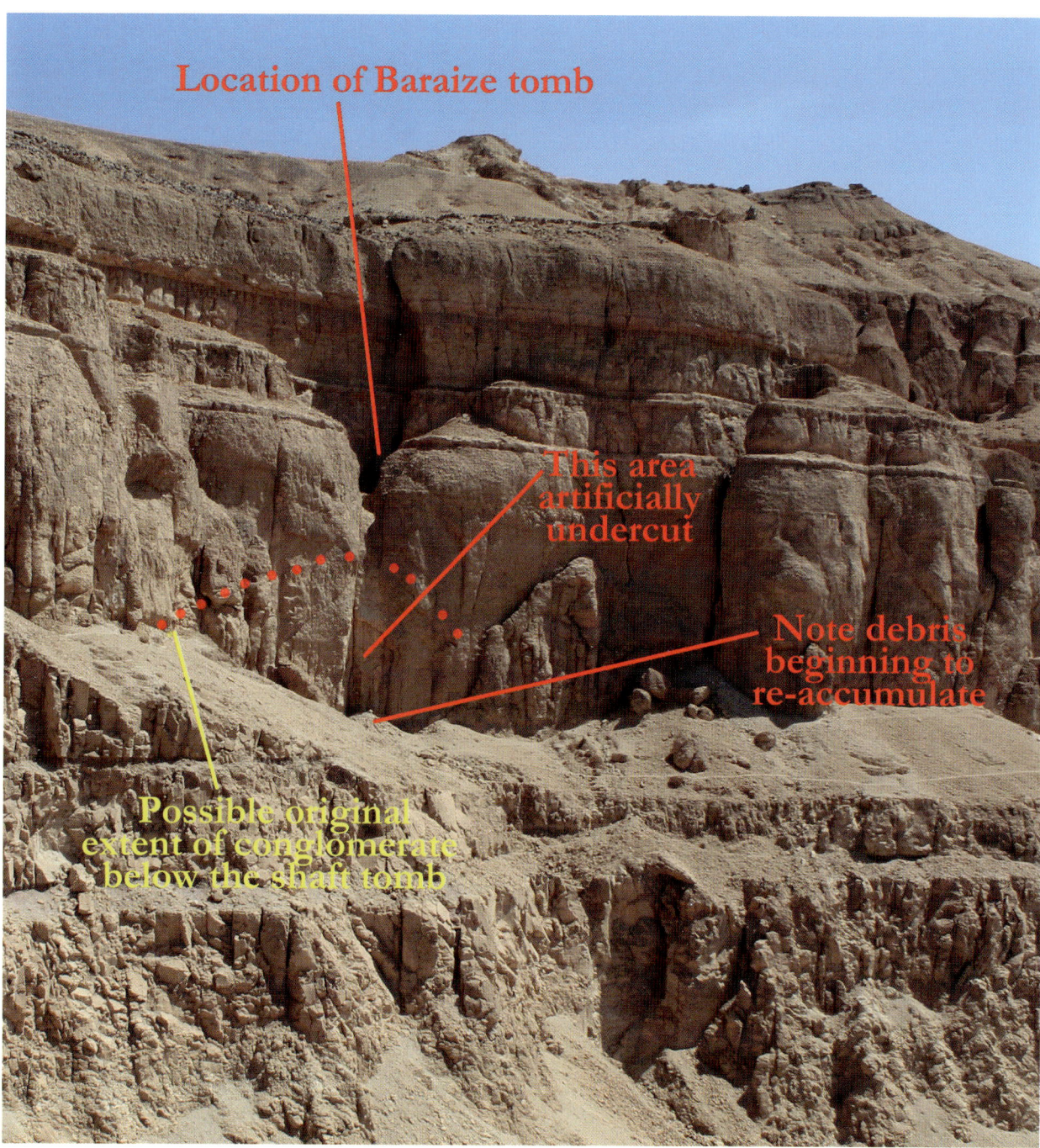

Figure 15. Baraize tomb location. Note small pile of water-borne debris starting to re-accumulate directly beneath the cliff-tomb crevice.

In the case of the Baraize cliff-tomb there appears to be the same artificial cutting-back of the cliff-face. There is less evidence of the remains of accumulated conglomerate but it seems highly likely that here again, access to the tomb site was facilitated by the shelf effectively being higher in ancient times. A large piece of rock which rests against the foot of the cliff may be associated with the movement of debris in ancient times. Certainly, below the Baraize tomb site there are signs of an accumulation of debris which seems to have originated on the shelf above the wadi floor.

Conclusions

Wadi A contains five known monuments (Carter's 20, 21, 22, 29 and the un-numbered shaft) *(Figure 9 and 16)*. There is a possibility of a further shaft-tomb hidden by debris at the very northern end (Carter's 23). Despite Carter's reputation for being methodical, the discrepancies between his unpublished notes and published maps sometimes suggests a degree of confusion. Carter may simply have misplaced 23.

In summary, there are two cliff-tombs, one associated with Hatshepsut, the other anonymous. There is one known shaft (Carter's 20) at the southern end of the wadi and there is one shaft with no chamber (Carter's 21) further north on the same terrace or shelf. It has been assumed that the second cliff-tomb and shafts are contemporary with Hatshepsut's cliff-tomb. However, all these tombs would benefit from further scrutiny. Shaft-tomb 20 has only ever been partially-cleared (Figure 18).

The rock-cut Coptic shelter low-down on the western side of the wadi would also benefit from further study.

Graffiti in the wadi appear to be mainly of XXth or early XXIst dynasty date and to relate to clearance of the wadi during that period. The enigmatic 'tomb graffiti' are impossible to date but indicate knowledge in ancient times of tombs or suitable tomb sites. It must remain an open question whether these were inscribed on the cliff walls by workmen indicating suitable sites for future work, or by the later teams scouring these wadis for burials to clear.

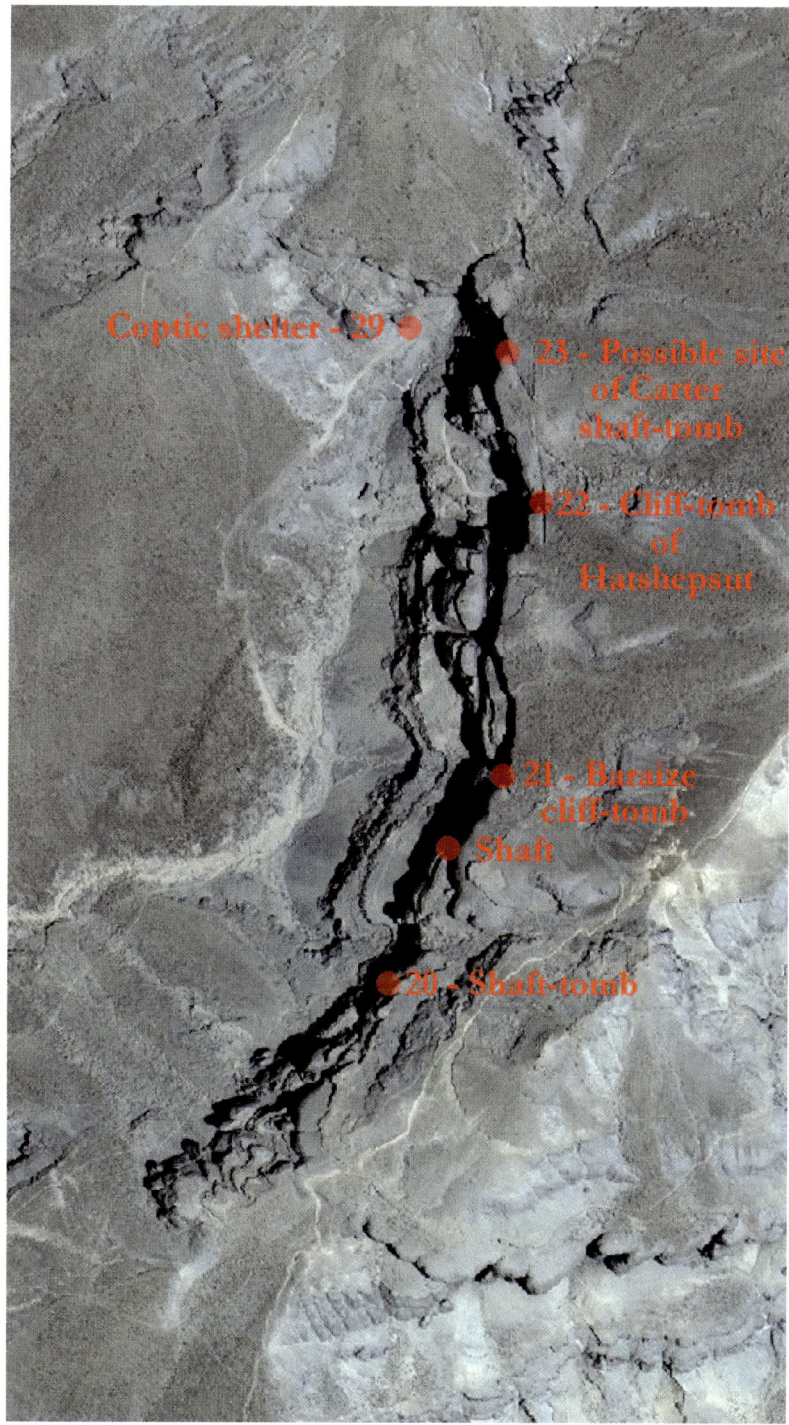

Figure 16. Satellite photograph oriented north showing positions of monuments in Wadi A.

Figure 17. Wadi A panorama showing major monuments and position of graffiti (G).

Figure 18. Interior of shaft-tomb 20 in Wadi A.

CHAPTER FIVE - Wadi C

Description

Wadi C is a bay which arcs to the east off the Wadi Gabbanat El-Qurud just to the north of Wadi B. It is formed by a single line of cliffs. A cliff tomb was cut into a natural crack in the rock three-quarters of the way up the bay, moving from south to north. This crack faces south and so, perhaps strangely, would have been obvious to anyone approaching along the wadi floor *(Figure 19)*. From above, on the cliff-top, the entrance to the tomb is all the more obvious *(Figure 20)*. It is not surprising, therefore, that this tomb was already empty when re-discovered by Carter in 1916.

Figure 19. The Wadi C bay with the cliff-tomb indicated.

Figure 20. The Wadi C cliff-tomb viewed from above.

Carter's findings

Carter drew a sketch map of the cliff-tomb *(Figure 20)* and on the basis of a graffito on a rock fifteen metres or so from the cliff face on the wadi floor, ascribed the tomb to Hatshepsut's daughter Nefrure. Carter and Thomas (the latter of whose assistants clearly entered the tomb)[16] note that this tomb was plastered with grey plaster but undecorated. Thomas notes that there were no visible artefacts in the tomb. The floor was covered in a layer of debris which, given the position of the tomb below a natural watercourse, and "the slight descent"[17] in the tomb floor, is likely to have been washed in.

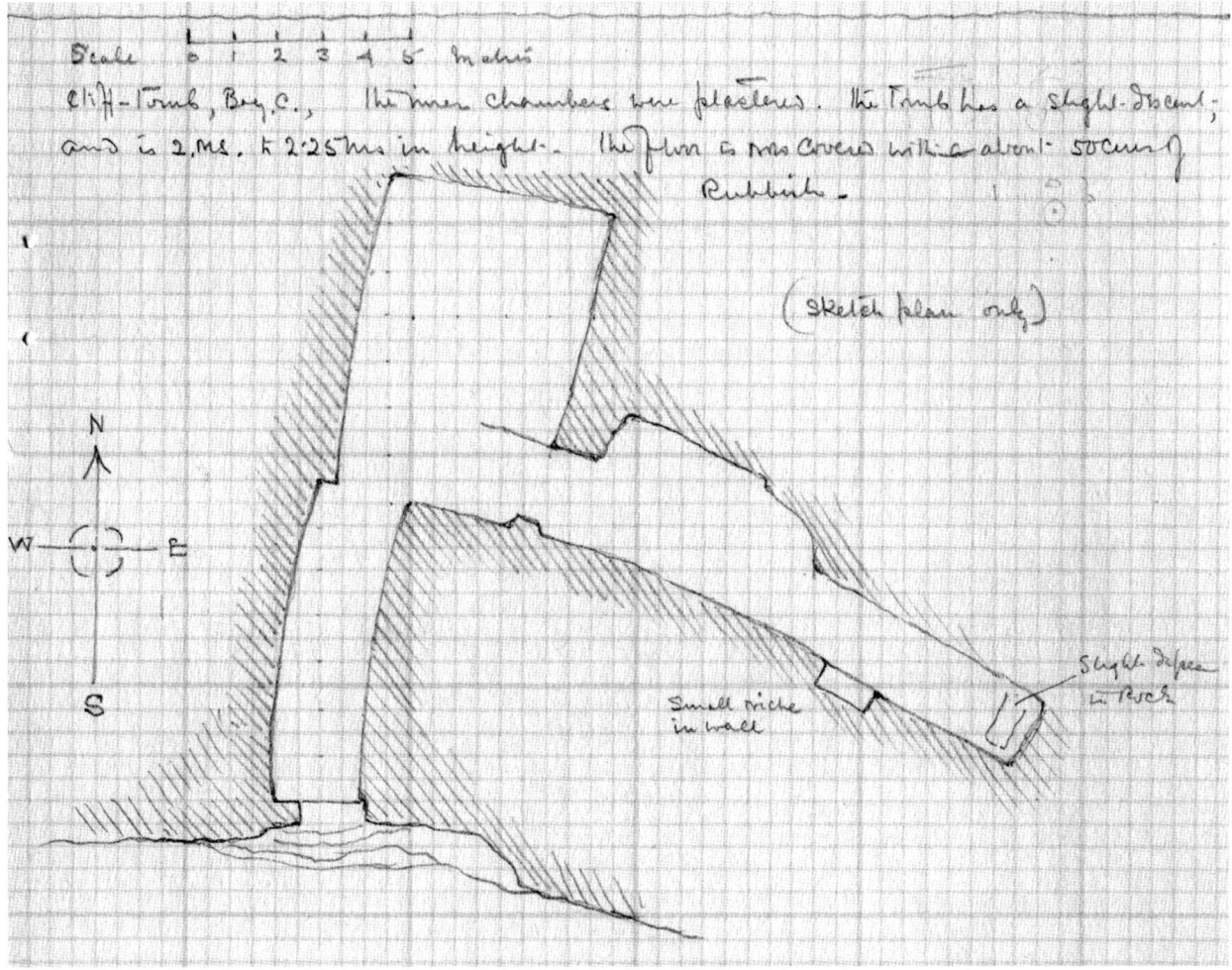

Figure 21. Carter's sketch plan of the cliff-tomb in Wadi C.

Carter's published map refers to three shaft tombs on the slope at the north of the wadi but his unpublished sketch map marks only two.

The wadi is inscribed with an extensive variety of graffiti not only on the cliff walls but also on the rocks at the foot of the cliff. Carter mentions only three graffiti, the Nefrure cartouche and two pharaonic inscriptions.

---

[16]Thomas, E. op. cit. p196.

[17]Carter, H. op. cit..

Černy and the CEDAE note a further twenty-six graffiti. Seven of these mention Butehamun, one mentions his father Djehutymose, one mentions his son, Ankhefenamun, one mentions Mehafto and two mention the Scribe in the Place of Truth, Nau-nedjem (or Nainudjem). The remaining fourteen which they note are either "pharaonic inscriptions" or "petroglyphs".

These graffiti are scattered along the foot of the cliff wall from a northern point immediately under the cliff-tomb to a point at the southern end of the bay on the far side of a natural water-course. Further out from the cliff-wall the large rocks which lie tumbled-to here are also covered in a wide variety of inscriptions. Some of these have been badly abraded by people walking over them and taking rubbing and squeezes. In some cases the Černy and CEDAE numbers have been lost.

Observations

Neither Elizabeth Thomas nor Jaroslav Černy was able to find the Nefrure cartouche. A photograph of it appears in Lilyquist[18] and it was spotted by our eagle-eyed inspector, Hanan Hassan Ahmed Hussein. It lies on top of a rock below and slightly to the south of the tomb crack and about fifteen metres away from the cliff-face. Interestingly, the cartouche is oriented towards the tomb. Its surface has deteriorated since Lilyquist photographed it. On Carter's sketch map of the wadi he records the "nefer" signs as occupying the whole of the lower part of the cartouche, there being no space for a determinative. Experimentation with various forms of raking light and a variety of

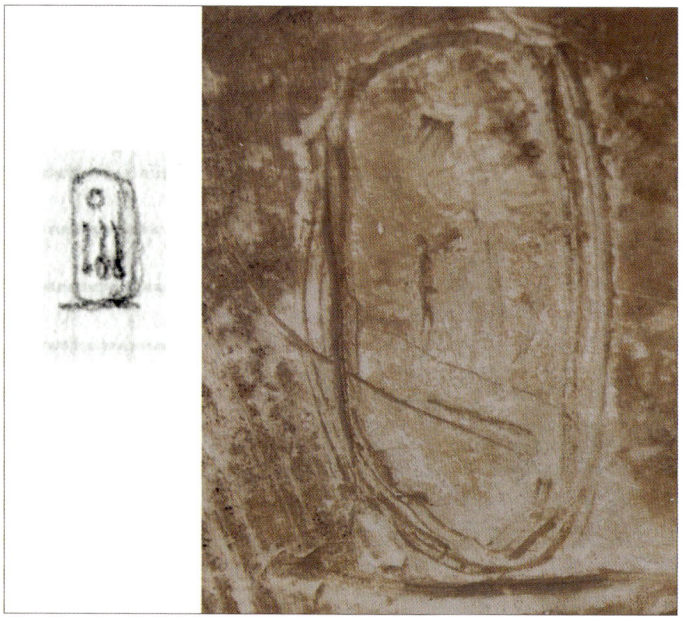

Figure 22. The "Nefrure" graffito as shown in Carter's notebook in the Griffith Institute and as photographed.

---

[18]Lilyquist, C. op. cit. p23 fig 9c.

photographic settings led Geoffrey Martin to conclude that this probably does read "Nefrure" *(Figure 21)*. The enclosure of the name in a cartouche narrows down the number of possibilities and no other known royal name accords with the discernible signs. This graffito is in poor condition and particularly vulnerable to pedestrian traffic.

Of the names included in the graffiti recorded here, Butehamun is again the most prominent and, once more it seems reasonable to assume, given the visible nature of the fissure into which the cliff-tomb was cut, that the presence of these late XXth and XXIst dynasty names relates to clearance work in this wadi. It is tempting to account for the quantity of graffiti by the quantity of burials in this area. Across on the western side of the wadi, and most often included as components of Wadi D, are seven open pit tombs which Carter described as lying open and rifled. They were assigned by Carter to apes. Of the pit-tombs Carter noted on the northern slope of Wadi C itself only two are visible today. He marks two on his unpublished map but refers to three in the 1917 JEA article. We were only able to find two and could only enter the westernmost of the two. This proved to be simply a shaft without a chamber. It is possible that Carter's reference to three shafts is a mistake.

Lying in amongst the debris below the cliff-tomb crack were several dressed, rectangular stones of a type used to seal tomb doors *(Figure 23)*. Another dressed blocking stone is visible in the entrance to the cliff-tomb *(Figure 24)*. These suggest that this tomb, unlike Hatshepsut's cliff tomb, was used for a burial - and the evidence of the cartouche does appear to point, literally, to this having been the XVIIIth dynasty burial of Nefrure *(Figure 22)*. It was again noted that the cutting of this cliff tomb had been facilitated by the presence of accumulated conglomerate at the base of the cliff. This remained in place on the left-hand side but had been removed immediately below and to the right of the tomb entrance. The large, remaining heap of this conglomerate is clearly visible. Once more the cliff face below the tomb has been cut away to make access more difficult *(Figure 25)*.

Figure 23. Blocking stones beneath the cliff-tomb in Wadi C.

Figure 24. Further blocking stone visible in the entrance to the Wadi C cliff-tomb.

Figure 25. Indications in red of possible size or original conglomerate pile, subsequently cut back except on the left. Yellow lines delineate area of cliff-face artificially cut away.

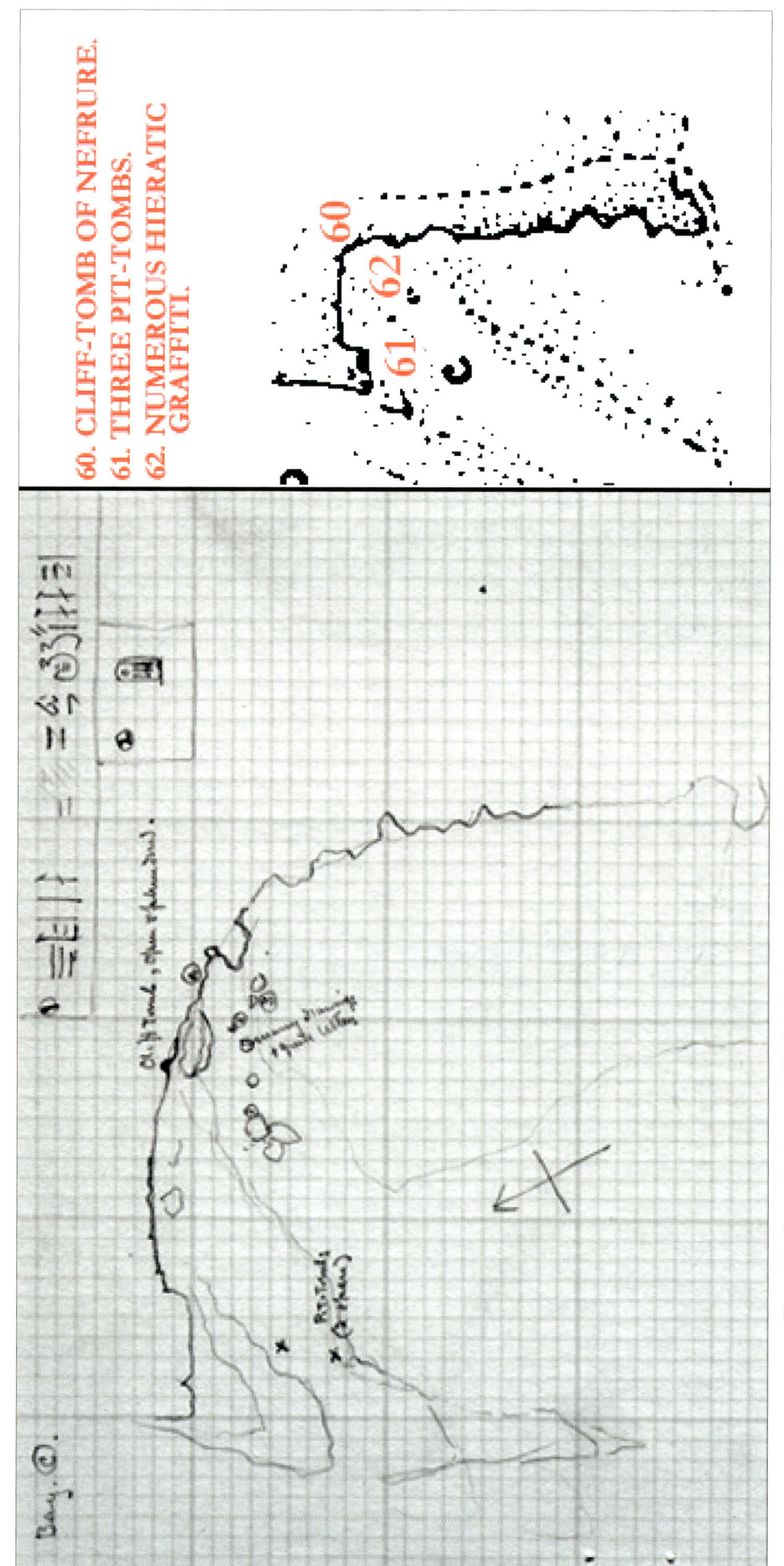

Figure 26. Carter sketch maps of Wadi C showing two pit-tombs in his Griffith Institute sketch-map (left) and three in the published sketch (right).

Figure 27. The two visible pit-tombs (shaft-tombs) on the northern slope of Wadi C.

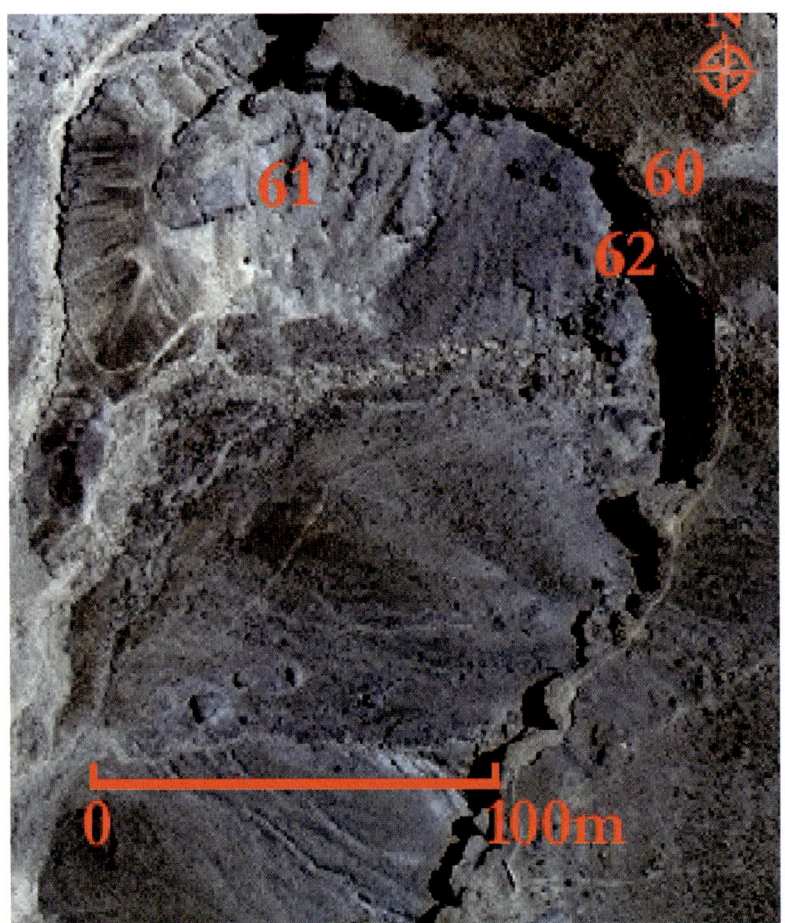

Figure 28. Satellite photograph of Wadi C, oriented north, showing Carter's number: 60 for the cliff-tomb, 61 for the pit- or shaft-tombs, and 62 for "numerous hieratic graffiti".

CHAPTER SIX - Wadi D

Description

Wadi D is formed by the V-shaped northern terminus of the Wadi Gabbanat El-Qurud *(Figure 29)*. As in Wadis B and C there is a single level of cliffs and these are broken at the northernmost point by a water-worn fissure which contains a shelf just under 8m above the wadi floor. Beyond, and to the north of this, there is a canyon and it was here, after the heavy rainfall of 1916 that a hitherto unplundered tomb came to light.

It is interesting, given the fact that this tomb remained intact, albeit heavily damaged by repeated flooding[19], that this wadi contains relatively few graffiti in the immediate vicinity of the tomb - in contrast to Wadi C, where the location of the cliff-tomb was most likely known in ancient times.

At the beginning of the wadi proper, on the eastern wall of the cliffs the name of Herihor appears. This is noteworthy as his name is otherwise associated exclusively with Wadi F.

There is a pit-tomb with stairs cut down into it at the foot of the eastern cliff wall 30m from the wadi-end, investigated and cleared by Lilyquist *(Figure 33)*. The graffiti again bear no relation to the location of this cache, possibly used for embalming materials. A second pit, noted by Lilyquist, has not been investigated and is nearer the Ankhefenamun and Nebhepe graffiti at the foot of the cliffs to the right of the shelf in which the cliff-tomb is hidden.

---

[19]Lilyquist, C. op. cit. p61.

Figure 29. Wadi D, the terminus of the Wadi Gabbanat El-Qurud. The tombs of the apes are distributed along the foot of the slope to the left just above the line of stones. The large, graffiti-covered rock is visible just left of centre.

Travelling south again, following the western walls of the wadi there is a small gulley about 50 metres south of the wadi end in which there are several graffiti. One of these graffiti names Butehamun.

Carter's findings

Further south still and on the sloping ground on the western side of the wadi a series of pit-tombs containing "the graves of apes, from which the valley derives its name"[20] were already lying open when Carter investigated the wadi and had been plundered in ancient times. On a large rock *(Figures 30 and 31)* to the east of these burials there is a quantity of mostly figurative graffiti. One of the names which appears on this rock, in abbreviated form, may be that of Dikhonsuiry who also appears in Wadi G.

Figure 30. Large graffiti-covered rock in the middle of Wadi D.

Figure 31. Figurative graffito on the large rock pictured in Figure 29 (digitally enhanced in red).

[20]Carter, H. op. cit. p110.

Observations

The overall dearth of graffiti here suggests, possibly, that work here during the period of clearances under Butehamun and others in the late XXth and early XXIst dynasties was concentrated in Wadi C and on the more superficial burials of apes south of the terminus of Wadi D.

Figure 32. Location of the Tomb of the Three Foreign Wives of Thutmose III and of the pit-tomb cleared by Lilyquist.

The major monument in this wadi, the cliff tomb of the three concubines or lesser wives of Thutmose III, survived undisturbed into modern times. This certainly lends encouragement to the view that there may still be undisturbed burials in these wadis. The tomb was cunningly concealed but was of a simple design. A flight of steps leads at right-angles to a descending corridor about 13m long oriented to the south-east. At the end of this corridor is a single burial chamber roughly 8m by 5m which turns to the right (south) *(Figure 33)*. The concealed position of the tomb in its ravine is reminiscent of that of Thutmose III's tomb in the Valley of the Kings. Unlike his tomb it was not protected (by a well chamber) against the floods which continued to pour periodically through the ravine and seep into the tomb. As a result water destroyed most of the soft items in the tomb leaving only the more durable to be robbed in 1916 as covered in Lilyquist[21].

---

[21] Lilyquist, C. op. cit.

The seven ape burials along the side of the wadi are now mostly blocked or badly eroded. One of the larger ones *(Figure 35)*, plastered with mud on the inside, has the beginnings of a shaft sunk in the floor. The work was apparently abandoned at the last minute as the flint pounders used to fracture the rock before it was chipped away are still in the depression (about 50cms in depth) which was all that was achieved of the shaft *(Figure 36)*. The meaning of these ape burials and the reason for their positioning remains unclear. It is not possible to say if they were associated with one particular private tomb in the vicinity or were more general in function. They are rougher versions of the animal burials found to the south-east of the tomb of Amenhotep II (KV35) in the Valley of the Kings.

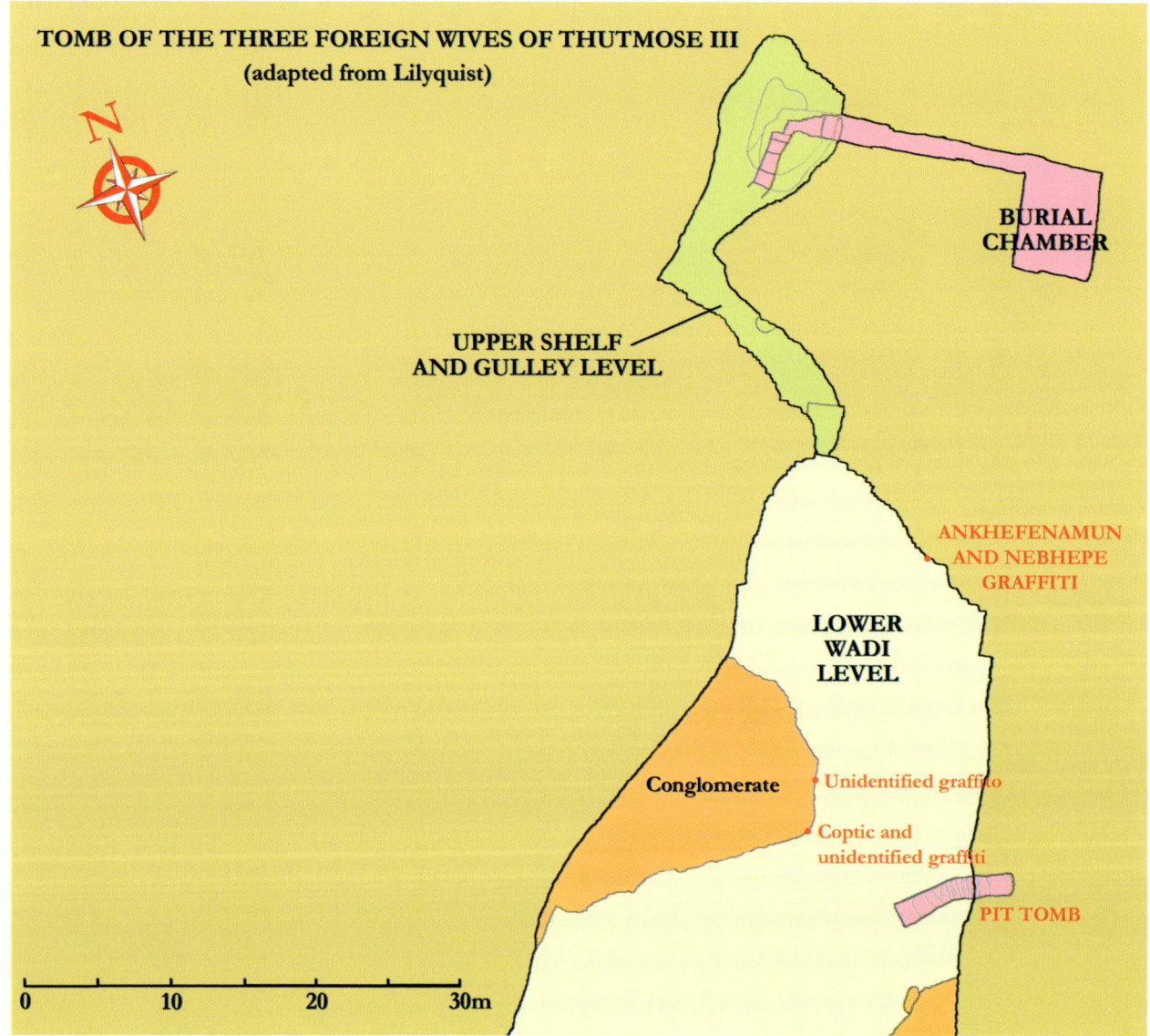

Figure 33. Plan of the Wadi D terminus showing the location of the main tomb and the subsidiary pit-tomb.

The shelf into which the cliff-tomb in Wadi D was excavated was, as in Wadis A and C, encumbered in pharaonic times with a pile of conglomerate which would have made access to the shelf much easier. On the left, western, side of the wadi this has been cut back some 14m from the rock cleft but a large pile still sits beyond that point on that side. On the right, or eastern, side of the wadi, the conglomerate has been cut back completely. The rock shelf itself shows signs, as in the case of Nefrure's cliff-tomb in Wadi C and the Baraize and Hatshepsut cliff-tombs in Wadi A, of being undercut to make access more difficult *(Figure 34)*. These features are, therefore, common to all the known cliff-tombs in these wadis.

Figure 34. The conglomerate body in Wadi D and the area cut away beneath the shelf.

Figure 35. One of the ape burials in Wadi D.

Figure 36. Interior of ape burial showing the commencement of a shaft with pounders left in place. These bear obvious percussion marks (as with the example in the bottom right of the photograph).

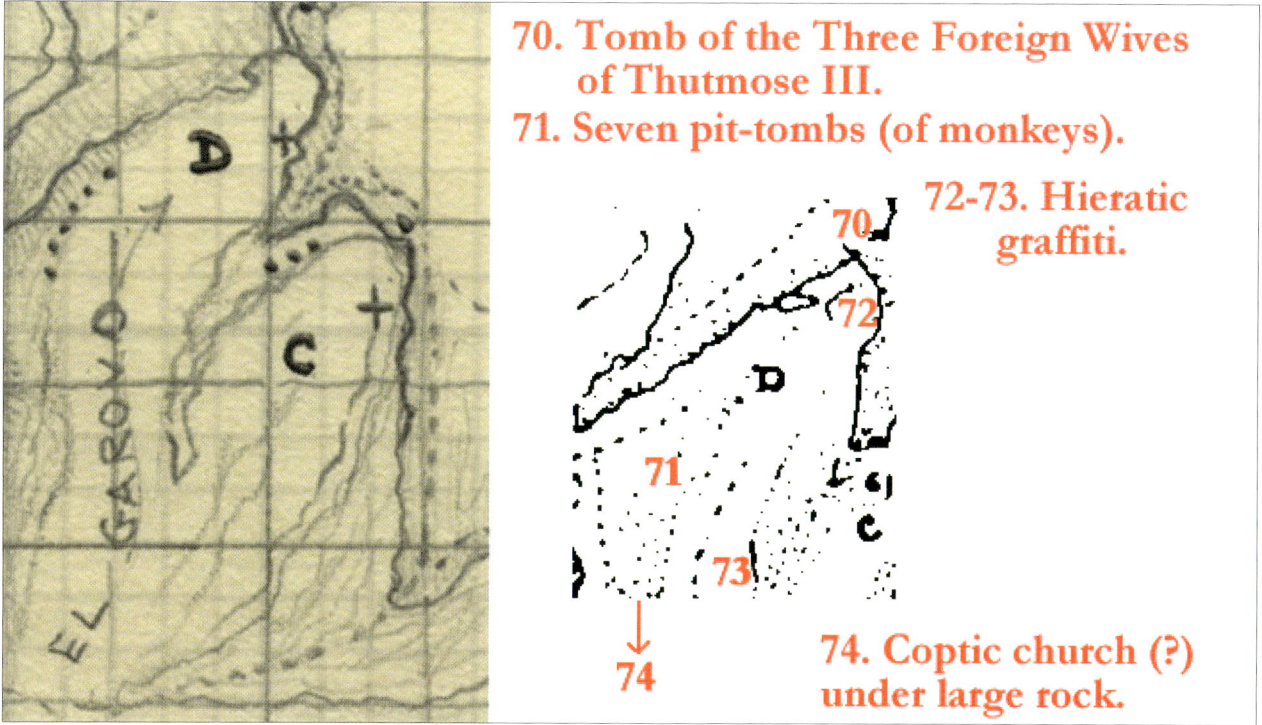

Figure 37. Carter's sketch map in the Griffith Institute on the left and the printed JEA article map on the right.

Carter mentions seven pit-tombs of monkeys but only marks six (as dots) on his sketch map. He marks three pit-tombs in Wadi C on the sketch map but on his other sketch map *(Figure 25)* says only two are open. Only two remain visible today *(see Figures 26 and 37)*.

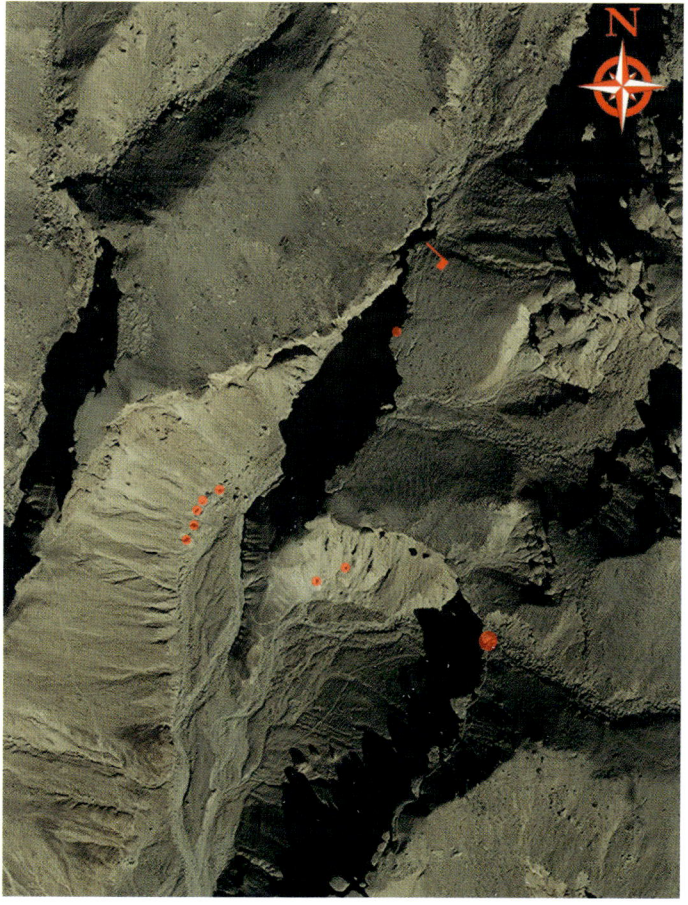

Figure 38. Location of the major monuments in Wadis C and D.

CHAPTER SEVEN - Wadi F

Figure 39. The approach to Wadi F.

Description

This is by far the largest and most complex of the Western Wadis. It is the furthest north and therefore the most remote. It consists, at it northern end, of four levels: one, steep scree slopes descending from the high desert at 500m; two, high cliffs descending from the bottom of these scree slopes; three a vast bowl some 650m by 450m at the base of these cliffs; four, a ravine cut in the bottom of this bowl which descends over what would once have been cascades, through a narrow gulley which is 10m wide in parts and 20m deep for much of its 200m length (Figures 40 and 41).

Carter's findings

Carter's maps tell slightly different stories about his view of this wadi (Figure 47) which contains by far the majority of the graffiti in all the wadis, a large proportion of which have not been recorded previously. Carter paid little attention to the graffiti possibly because he intended to return to the wadi.

Much attention has been paid to this wadi and its potential because Carter believed there to be tombs here. The availability of the Valley of the Kings concession after the First World War and his subsequent discovery of KV62 meant that he never returned to work here. His evidence in support of the possible presence of tombs, which has been much repeated and, indeed, augmented, was expressed as follows:

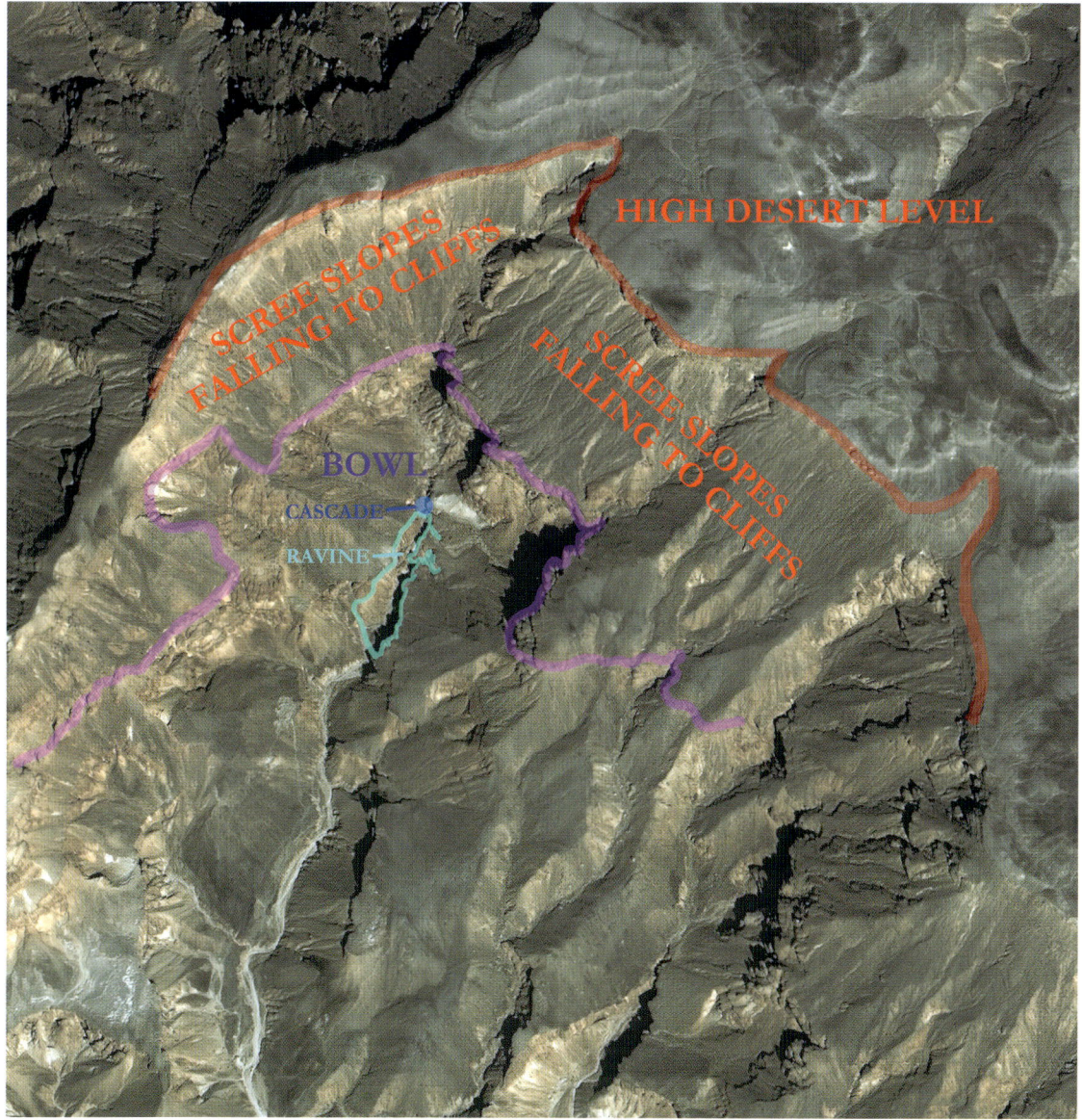

Figure 40. The complex structure of Wadi F.

a) "stone chippings from some ancient excavation" (in the floor of the wadi; 101 in his published map);

b) "stone huts of workmen" (in a side wadi opposite the ancient excavations; 102 in his published map);

c) "heaps of ancient origin" (higher up the wadi, to the north, above the "cascade"; 100 in his published map);

d) "The graffiti and heaps of rubbish indicate the presence of tombs in the vicinity, as the natives have long recognised; but the extensive excavations made by them have been apparently without result."

e) "I am making more extensive soundings here in the hope of revealing lost tombs. I have already found a piece of crystalline sandstone from a sarcophagus - the projection for the levers used in transportation."

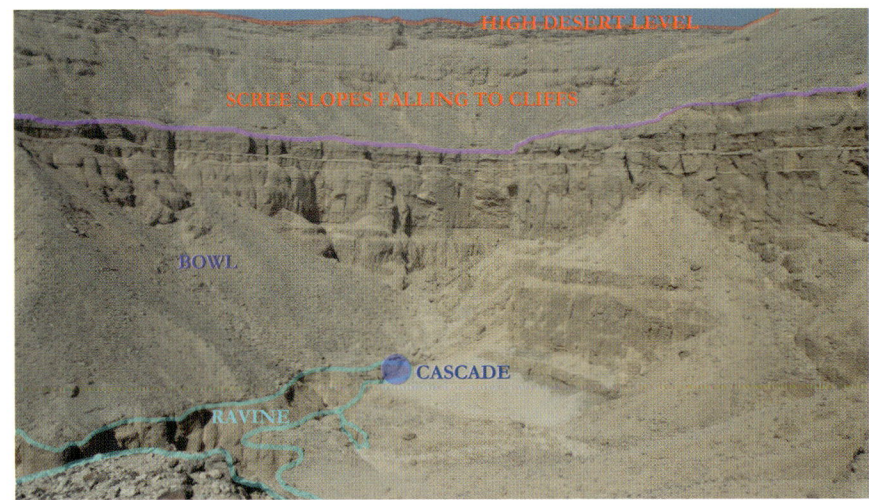

Figure 41. Wadi F general view of topography.

Figure 42. View of the entrance to the ravine showing the complex nature of the site.

Figure 43. The bowl and ravine in Wadi F looking south from above the cascade.

Figure 44. The ravine, looking south.

Figure 45. Excavations in the ravine in Wadi F opposite the site of the workmen's settlement. These excavations most likely pre-date Howard Carter's inspection of the wadi.

Figure 46. The cascade in Wadi F with the large blocks noted by Carter both above and below the cascade.

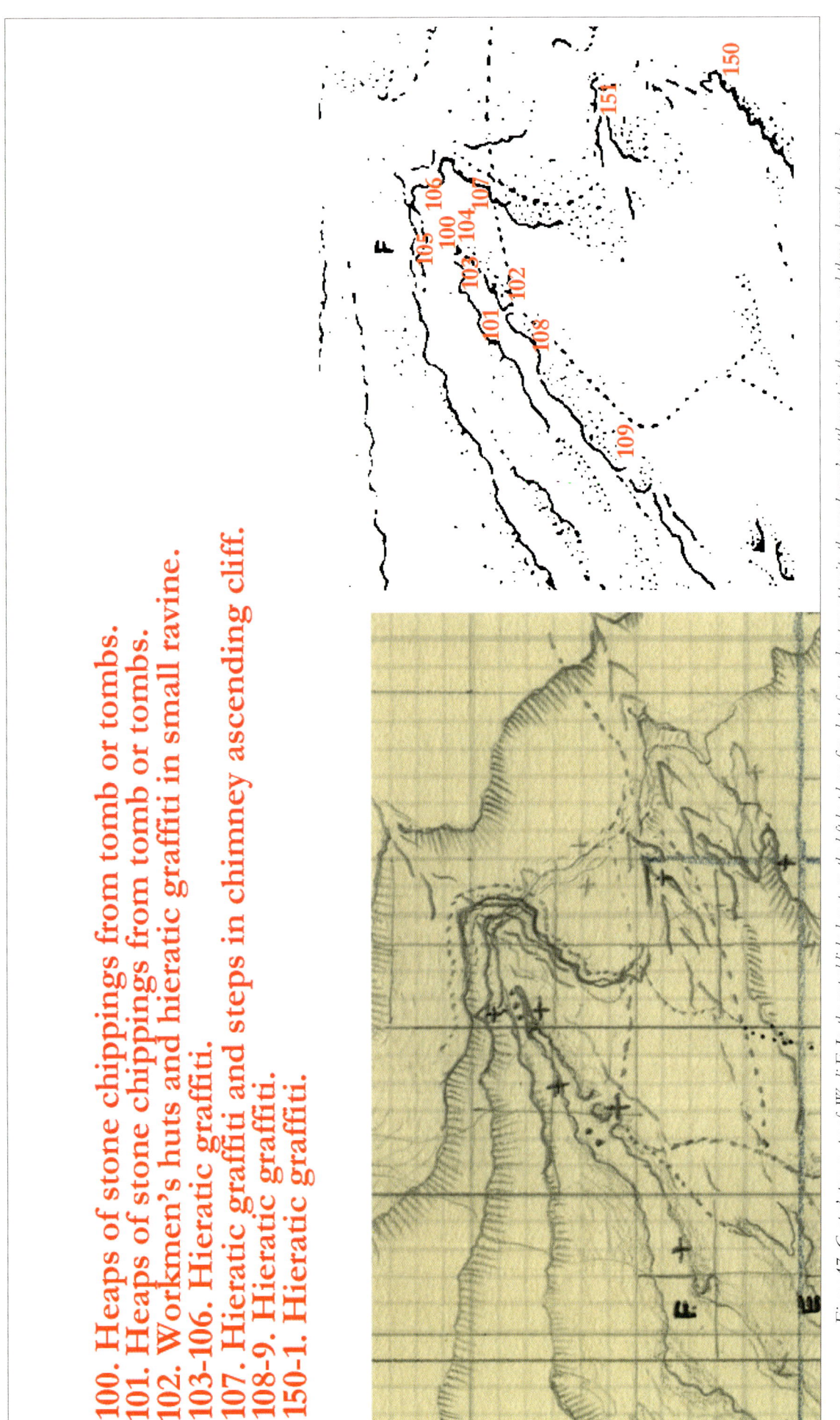

100. Heaps of stone chippings from tomb or tombs.
101. Heaps of stone chippings from tomb or tombs.
102. Workmen's huts and hieratic graffiti in small ravine.
103-106. Hieratic graffiti.
107. Hieratic graffiti and steps in chimney ascending cliff.
108-9. Hieratic graffiti.
150-1. Hieratic graffiti.

Figure 47. Carter's two maps of Wadi F. In the unpublished map on the left he places five dots for tombs, two opposite the workmen's settlement in the ravine and three above the cascade where he believed he had found piles of stone chippings.

The Western Wadis of the Theban Necropolis

It is important to recognise that most of the excavations which have taken place in this wadi were conducted either in ancient times or by illicit digging in the last 150 years or so. Carter's own work in these wadis was relatively limited and may consist simply in the sondages visible in two locations *(Figure 48)*. It is also important to note that Carter records finding a single fragment of a sarcophagus, not four. Identification of this fragment has not been confirmed.

Figure 48. Sondages, top, in the ravine just south of the workmen's settlement site and, bottom, high on the western side of the wadi. These were probably made by Carter.

Carter's sketch maps *(Figure 47)* show that he believed there to be at least five tombs here, two under the spoil-heaps in the narrow ravine opposite the settlement site and three higher up next to the other, larger spoil-heaps he identified above the waterfall.

This wadi contains seventy-six recorded groups of graffiti and during the course of our investigations we found what are almost certainly additional graffiti in thirty-nine groups. These consist of a variety of types ranging from indecipherable scratches to arrows, hieratic inscriptions and faces. These graffiti are in three principal types of locations: in the narrow ravine at the lowest level south of the cascade; above the cascade, principally on the eastern side of the bowl; and on the cliff walls.

Figure 49. The pile of "rubbish" which Carter believed to be composed of stone chippings.
It is in fact composed of naturally-formed debris washed down the wadi from above and eroded at the margins by subsequent flows of water.

Those in the narrow ravine are found where there were settlements in ancient times. The remains of huts, much disturbed, survive in several locations in the ravine and seem to be of a type common throughout the Theban necropoleis and indicative of tomb-building or the policing of tombs. With few exceptions these 'settlements' seem to have been temporary, used possibly for a matter of weeks at a time and then abandoned once the tombs were built.

The graffiti here seem to fall into two time periods. There are graffiti of the XVIIIth dynasty, including the two cartouches of Amenhotep II (3883 in the Graffiti de la Montagne Thebaine - GMT[22]), *(Figure 50)* and the now almost invisible striding figure bearing the praenomen of Thutmose III and the title *neb tawy*[23]. This was virtually impossible to discern even with the naked eye (3884 in the GMT).

---

[22]Černy, J. et al 1969-1983 'Graffiti de la Montagne Thebaine' 4 volumes, CEDAE, Le Caire.

[23]Peden, A. 2001 'The Graffiti of Pharaonic Egypt', Brill, Leiden, Boston, Cologne. p145.

Figure 50. The 3883 Amenhotep II graffito in the workmen's settlement off the ravine in Wadi F.

Given the activity in neighbouring wadis A, C and D in the XVIIIth dynasty, there can be no reason why burials of the XVIIIth dynasty should not have been located also in Wadi F. The existence of XVIIIth dynasty burials even further afield (see WB1 below) makes such activity likely. It also seems fair to assume that the presence of the familiar crew bearing names such as Butehamun and Djehutymose and other names such as Montuseankh, indicates a second phase of activity in the late XXth or early XXIst dynasty devoted to the extraction of XVIIIth dynasty burials still hidden here.

Observations - Herihor

Herihor's name appears here five times. It has been suggested that this is indicative of a burial of Herihor in this wadi and, possibly, the burials of some of his successors. The spoil-heaps and other evidence for tombs which Carter identified are proposed as evidence of the excavation of a large, new tomb for these rulers of Upper Egypt[24].

There are several problems raised by this suggestion:

1. There is good evidence, which is widely accepted, that Butehamun and his men were involved in inspecting, extracting and consolidating royal burials of earlier periods nearer the centres of administration during the rule of Herihor[25]. The royal caches (DB320, KV35 and, possibly, KV40) demonstrate a preference for more concentrated re-burials in places which could be easily monitored.

2. The debris opposite the "settlement" in the ravine in Wadi Γ is water-borne sediment which was washed down in prehistoric times and which was disturbed by excavation before Carter inspected these wadis, as he records.

3. According to our geologists the larger piles of stone chippings, above the cascade, are composed of natural debris borne down from the upper part of the wadi by ancient flooding. They have been eroded on both sides by water flows subsequent to their formation and therefore have the appearance of being man-made. Flakes which fall from the cliffs fracture in the same way as flakes chipped from tomb-cutting. It is characteristic of limestone to break up in this way (as the builders of tombs knew). Only the presence of tell-tale chisel marks on flakes confirms that they were extracted during tomb construction. None of the accessible flakes in these piles bears chisel marks. It is therefore highly unlikely that Carter was right about these being piles of debris extracted from tombs.

4. Carter's evidence therefore comes down to two things: the presence of workmen's huts and the single sarcophagus boss[26] he uncovered. There is nothing to relate this boss to the Third Intermediate Period and whilst it was unusual for royal women to have stone sarcophagi, the one example of such a sarcophagus prepared for a woman is in another of the Western Wadis and dates to the XVIIIth dynasty.

5. Where Herihor's name appears in this wadi, it appears without cartouches. If he was, indeed, buried here, it would be unthinkable that his name would be expressed without respect for the position to which he aspired at the end of his rule - namely that of a king.

---

[24]Romer, J. 1984 'Ancient Lives', Michael O'Mara Books Ltd, London. pp195-9; Peden, A. op. cit. pp232-7 and Peden, A. in Lilyquist op.cit. pp7-12.

[25]Reeves, C.N. op. cit. pp233-237.

[26]Carter is specific in mentioning only one sarcophagus boss. This has become "bosses" in Romer, J. op. cit. pp195-9 and "four crystalline sandstone bosses" in Peden op. cit. pp 232-7.

6. None of the other XXth dynasty and XXIst dynasty names are indicative of the burial of the individuals named in the wadis in which they appear.

7. The appearance of Herihor's name in Wadi D does not suggest he was buried there. In isolation, therefore, the appearance of Herihor's name does not seem to provide evidence of his burial in this location.

The presence of XVIIIth dynasty names in a wadi which, for all that it is more remote, is still connected with wadis A, B, C, D, E and G by ancient pathways, is highly suggestive of burial activity in that period. No persuasive argument has yet been advanced to account for the presence of XVIIIth dynasty kings' names in any other way. Nor, indeed, has any persuasive argument been advanced to explain why Butehamun and his gangs were, apparently in this wadi alone, suddenly tomb-builders and not tomb-clearers.

A final problem with the hypothesis that Herihor is buried in Wadi F is that locating Herihor's burial in a remote wadi during a time of apparent insecurity runs counter to the overall direction in which burials seem to have taken place from the late XVIIIth dynasty onwards.

In the XIXth dynasty royal family burials were brought back into the more centrally-situated 'Valley of the Queens'; subsequent movements of royal burial contents, and most specifically, the royal bodies, were centripetal. Would Herihor have regarded Wadi F as more secure than, for example, the DB320 royal cache complex, when his own workforce in the main royal necropolis and adjacent wadis had demonstrated with their clearances the vulnerability of the Western Wadis?

As noted, Wadi F is a very difficult and very large site. Carter thought there were tombs in the ravine opposite the workmen's 'settlement' and tombs may well exist here in amongst the large rocks which clutter the wadi floor. If they do, they are as likely to be the tombs of members of the XVIIIth dynasty royal family as of any other period. Known burial activity in these wadis, and beyond, supports this view. Carter also was in error when he posited tombs above the cascade from the presence of apparent spoil-heaps. He was wrong about the spoil-heaps.

There may well be tombs hidden in the surrounding cliffs. Two caveats need to be observed, however. The rock down the western side of the bowl in Wadi F is heavily fractured both horizontally and vertically.

It does not look like the sort of rock which ancient workmen would have made a priority for tomb location. Secondly, if cliff-tombs are to be found it is likely that they will be in places where the natural conglomerate accumulations have been used to gain access to burial places and subsequently cut away (as in Wadis A, C and D). The best of these sites are on the west of the wadi bowl.

Observations - General

One of the curious features of this wadi is the choice of settlement site. There is, off the north-eastern end of the ravine, below the cascade, a thin but commodious (20m by 3m) side-ravine which is almost completely closed-off where it joins the main ravine. It would have offered almost complete security against wild animals, protection from the wind and would have been ideal for storage. It has a small entrance just big enough to allow one person to enter at a time. Carter noted one graffito on a rock just outside the entrance but the present expedition failed to locate it. The side-ravine itself contains no graffiti of any sort and no signs of ever having been utilised. It may have been completely blocked in ancient times.

There are the remains of huts just to the north on this eastern side and there are the remains of huts in the larger, cup-like wadi further south *(Figure 51)*. This latter side-wadi gives easier access than the cascade route to the bowl level of Wadi F and there is a path which leads up the cliff level and to the foot of what Carter identified as a staircase in the rock. These staircases, or short-cuts through the cliffs, are not unusual in the Theban Massif cliffs. This one is blocked and must at some stage have had an artificial step to allow access at the bottom as the shelf there is too high to climb unaided. It is unclear where this staircase emerges as there is no fissure in the rock in the position shown by Carter which leads to the top of the cliffs. All the possible candidates stop short of the cliff-top *(Figure 52)*.

Figure 51. The cup-like side-wadi off the main ravine where there are ancient huts.

Figure 52. Possible route from the workmen's settlement to the east of the ravine up to the "staircase" in the cliffs.

At the top of the cliffs there are several huts and a pathway which leads up to the high desert road. Carter shows this to the north of the gulley but the path we followed was to the south. This southern route was exceptionally steep and impossible to use in places without the use of one's hands.

We could find no evidence of water-gathering or storage at the high desert level. What appeared to be possible reservoirs or wells on satellite photographs proved to be excavations for quartzite or gypsum. There is no doubt that pathways from the wadis below connect with the high desert road but the inclines involved in ascending and descending these routes must raise some doubt about their use as supply routes to those camped below.

Figure 53. Entrance to the "staircase". The step up is about 2m high.

Figure 54. Looking up the "staircase" from the bottom.

Figure 55. Possible routes out of Wadi F onto the high desert.

CHAPTER EIGHT - Wadi G

Description

Wadi G is the most westerly of the Western Wadis but opens off the Wadi El-Gharby some 875m south of the part of that wadi designated Wadi F by Carter. Wadi G heads west and then turns north, splitting into two smaller wadis either side of a central tongue. It is bounded on all but its south-eastern side by a circular bay of cliffs roughly 70m in height *(Figure 56)*.

Figure 56. Wadi G. Photograph oriented to the north.

Carter drew several sketches of this wadi and interpretation of these has led to some confusion. Elizabeth Thomas took his sketch marked "TONGUE"[27] *(Figure 57)*, to refer to the broad slope which descends from the eastern heights of Wadi G and separates it from the main Wadi El-Gharby. The sketch in fact refers to an area immediately to the west of the main central tongue of Wadi G *(Figure 58)* where Carter noted the presence of three shaft tombs and a possible cliff tomb (marked 127 on figure 57).

---

[27]Thomas, E. op. cit. p199 middle, right.

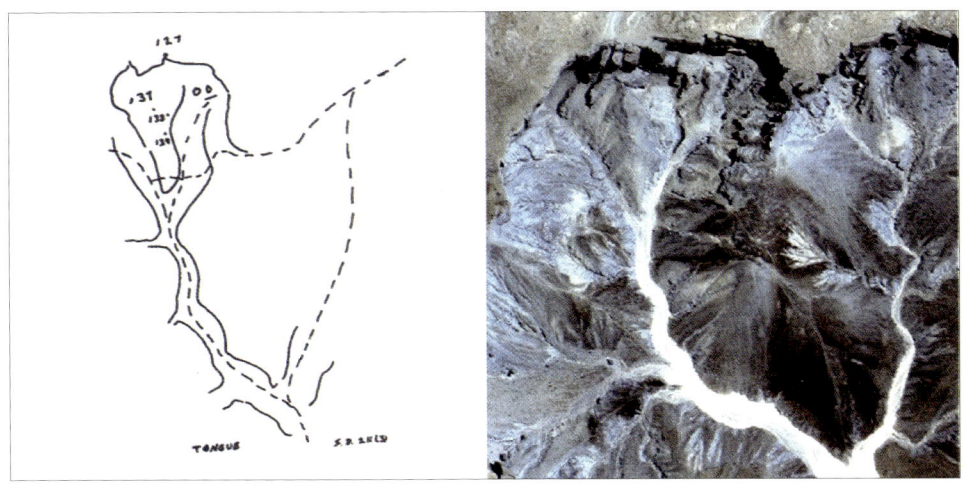

Figure 57. Carter's "tongue" sketch which relates to the small tongue to the east of the large central one.

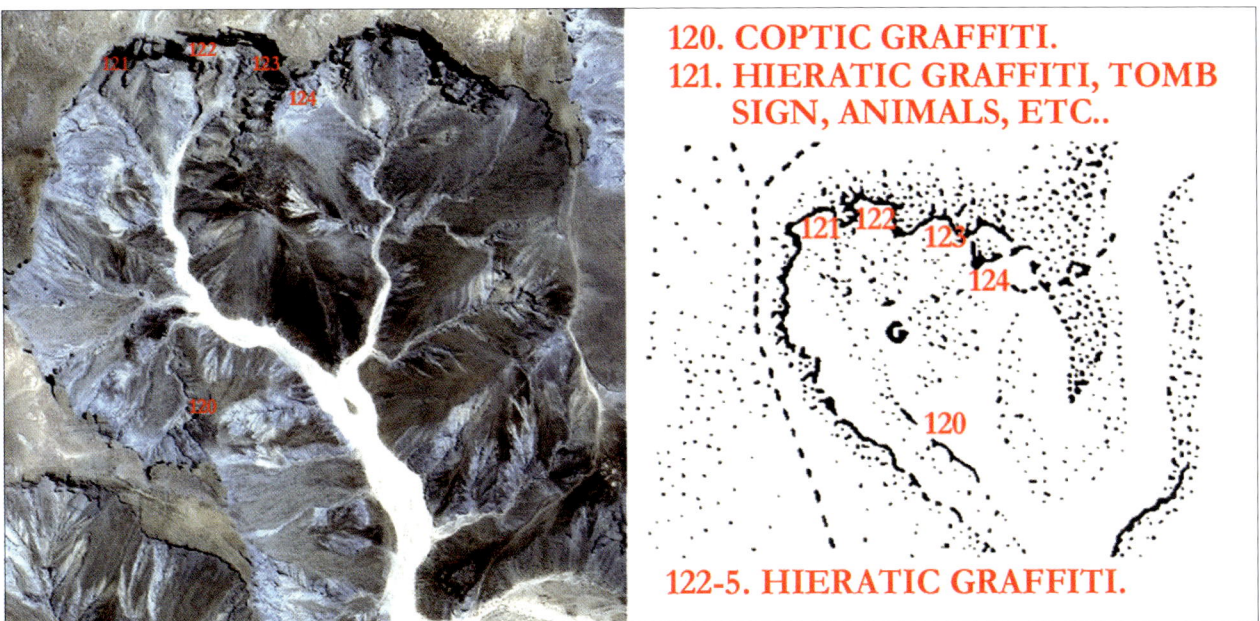

Figure 58. Carter's published sketch of Wadi G with numbers transferred to satellite photograph on left.

This area is where the the main concentration of graffiti occurs. There is a deep cleft in the cliffs here which forms a natural shelter. Judging by the animal graffiti here and in the smaller recess in the cliffs to the west this was used in prehistoric times. An abundance of Coptic graffiti here indicates usage in that period.

At the eastern end of this natural cleft there is a rock shelf some 7.5m above the floor of the cleft. Carter marks this as a likely site (127) for a cliff-tomb in his Griffith Institute notes *(Figure 57)*. Inspection of the rock face under this shelf revealed a graffito, marked in a blue pencil similar to that used in Carter's sketch map *(Figure 2, Figure 61)*. The graffito is a 'tomb' sign.

On the tongue to the south of this cleft Carter marks three shaft- or pit-tombs, one of which is open at the moment and has been used by animals recently *(Figure 61)*. Of the other two there is now no sign.

Figure 59. The Wadi G 127 niche.

Figure 60. the shelf at the western end of the Wadi G 127 niche.

On the plateau above the cliffs to the north of Wadi G there has been extensive mining activity, presumably for gypsum, but possibly also for flints. There is some evidence, much disturbed, of settlements here and the quantity of flint debitage suggests use of these cliff-tops in prehistoric times.

Graffiti

The graffiti in this wadi names only one individual, Dikhonsuiry. His name appears three times, twice in the same small area where the prehistoric giraffes and ostriches are located (Carter's 121) and once to the east of the central tongue. The remainder of the graffiti are figurative and predominantly Coptic.

*Figure 61. The Wadi G 127 niche just right of centre.
To the left of that, just below the centre of the photograph is a small opening which Carter marked as one of three pit-tombs.*

Observations

The 127 cleft remains intriguing. The rock under the shelf has been cut back artificially. There is an accumulation of conglomerate which seems to have been cut back from the cliff face *(Figures 59 and 62)*. In these respects the site conforms with the sites of the other cliff-tombs.

The presence of the tomb sign beneath the shelf tempts one to believe, as Carter clearly did, that there is a cliff tomb here. It is extremely difficult to obtain a view of the top of the shelf. The photographs we were able to take reveal a shelf covered to a depth of about 15cms with bird droppings which obscure the surface beneath just sufficiently to make the underlying topography unclear. Our photographs are foreshortened but the space here looks to be approximately 1.8m deep and between 90cms and 1m wide. This is very restricted for a tomb opening and so the chances of one existing on this shelf seem marginal. The crevice in this cleft continues westwards and there is a small chance of something being concealed at the western end of the fracture. Two tomb signs engraved on the rock below encourage that view.

The shaft tomb visible to the south of the 127 cleft *(Figure 61)* would benefit from clearance and a more thorough search of that tongue might well reveal the other two shafts marked by Carter.

The Western Wadis of the Theban Necropolis

Figure 62. Wadi G 127 niche.

Figure 63. The tomb sign in the Wadi G 127 niche The photograph has been digitally enhanced to show the sign in red. Note also the blue pencil - similar to that used by Carter on his sketch map - which has been used to outline the graffito here.

Figure 62. Wadi G 127 niche.

Figure 63. The tomb sign in the Wadi G 127 niche The photograph has been digitally enhanced to show the sign in red. Note also the blue pencil - similar to that used by Carter on his sketch map - which has been used to outline the graffito here.

CHAPTER NINE - Wadi B and Wadi E

Wadi B

Description

Wadi B is a tributary of the Wadi Gabbanat El-Qurud and opens to the east of that wadi about 300m further north of the the Wadi Sikket Taqet Zaid. It runs east-west and is walled to the south by a single height of cliffs cut at the eastern end by a deep, water-worn gulley. To the north the cliffs are replaced by steep scree slopes *(Figure 64 and 65)*.

Figure 64. The end of Wadi B looking east.

Figure 65. Wadi B from above looking south-east.

Carter's findings

The wadi appears to contain just one group of six Coptic graffiti, noted by Carter and recorded by the CEDAE as 3961-3966. We found no evidence of burial activity in this wadi and none was found by Elizabeth Thomas[28].

---

[28]Thomas, E. op. cit. p196.

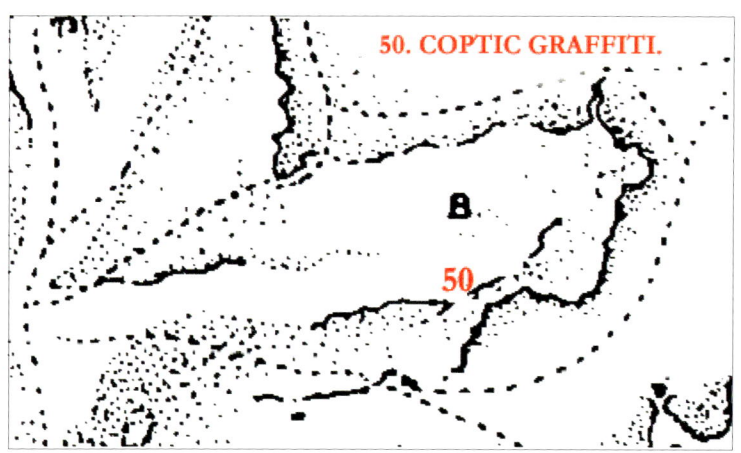
Figure 66. Carter's published map of Wadi B marking just the site of Coptic graffiti.

Observations

The assumption that this wadi contains no burials appears to be based on the absence of graffiti. If graffiti of the XXth and XXIst dynasties relate to clearances of known tombs it is possible that there are unknown tombs in this wadi which only a systematic archaeological clearance of the wadi would reveal.

Wadi E

Description

This area is less a real wadi than a bay in the Wadi El-Gharby. It lies some 400m to the south of Wadi F and 400m to the north of Wadi G.

Carter's findings

Wadi E contained nothing of interest to Carter but it lies immediately under, and to the north of, an eminence, forming the eastern side of the wadi, on which in pharaonic times there was a guard post or settlement of sorts (95 on Carter's published JEA map[29]).

Observations

The position of these huts would have given a view over the approaches to all seven of the wadis Carter covered in his 1917 article.

---

[29] Carter, H. op. cit..

CHAPTER TEN - Wadi Bariya Site 1 (WB1)

Carter's findings

In his 1917 JEA article[30], Carter mentions a site outside the circle of wadis to which he gave the letters A to G. The following is his description:

"Opposite the entrance [to the Wadi Sikket el Agala] and a few hundred metres out into the plain is a small piece of rising ground where there are five open pit-tombs, which have been plundered in both ancient and modern times. They appear to have been royal, for a fragment of an alabaster Canopic jar (burnt) bears the beginning of the word for king ⸻ a part of the human-headed lid is of the finest workmanship, and from the pot-sherds around the mouths of these pits - of the finest grey earthenware - one would claim them to be of the period of Amenophis III. Higher up on the rising ground are many stone huts of the type adapted to workmen. A large, wide road crosses the plain below these remains and, at a sharp bend, enters the valley, where it continues up the great northern arm, but how far I have so far been unable to ascertain."

Carter displays a curious lack of interest in these five "pit-tombs" - despite their possibly being royal, and despite their containing artefacts said to be of the highest workmanship dating, apparently, from a reign which witnessed one of the high points of pharaonic artistry.

From Carter's description it is not clear what he thinks constitutes the entrance to the Wadi El-Agala. There is a T-junction at the southern end of this wadi which might qualify as the entrance. However, perusal of satellite photographs and Google Earth revealed five dark pits on a low piece of ground on the western side of the Wadi Bariya, opposite the point at which the Wadi El-Agala opens finally onto the Wadi Bariya. The site is completely exposed. There are no clefts or hiding places on the low and largely flat plateau which is elevated a mere ten to fifteen metres above the Wadi Bariya floor. Any work done here, whether in connection with the original excavation or subsequent robberies, would have been visible to anyone on the higher ground not only of the main Theban Massif to the east but of higher ground to the north-west.

We visited this site with our inspector, Hanan Hassan Ahmed Hussein, and four guards who claimed to be familiar with the site "where one tomb leads to the next".

---

[30]Carter, H. op. cit..

Figure 67. The exposed site WB1, opposite the point at which the Wadi El-Agala empties onto the broad floodplain of the Wadi Bariya.

Our truck was unable to make much progress up the sandy bed of the Wadi Bariya and so we walked the last two kilometres, hugging the eastern side of the Wadi Bariya and then cutting across to the rising ground just before the entrance to the Wadi El-Agala *(Figure 70)*. Some two hundred metres from the foot of the rising ground there was a blocking stone and near that a second. A third blocking stone lying near the second was broken in half.

Figure 68. Blocking stone on the wadi floor. A4 file for scale.

Along the foot of the rising ground there were workmen's huts in several separate groups. Judging by the depth of the bottom layer of stones these were of ancient origin.

Figure 69. Hut in foreground at the foot of the rising ground. Figures on the horizon are next to the shaft-tombs.

Figure 70. Further huts lining the foot of the rising ground.

The path leading up the slope was well-worn and littered with broken pottery of a variety of types ranging from unglazed terracotta to thin-bodied glazed ware. The spoil heaps round the various "pit-tombs" were large and obvious. Two of the smaller pits were blocked but the three larger ones were either open or partially open *(Figure 73)*.

With some difficulty given the friability of the gravelly layer of conglomerate which formed the upper stratum, two of us inspected the least encumbered of the shafts (the westernmost of the larger shafts) expecting to find a single chamber at the bottom cut into the underlying limestone bedrock.

Figure 71. Broken pottery on the path up the slope.

The bottom of the shaft (1.5m by 3m and possibly 8m deep) was filled with debris allowing crawling room only into the rooms off the shaft. There were rooms off both the northern and southern ends of the shaft.

Figure 72. The site looking south towards Medinet Habu and the Nile.

The northern room (A) was roughly 4m wide by 5m long and the small room off its northern end (Aa), accessed by a door just over a metre wide, was 3.3m wide by 2.3 m long.

Off the main northern room to the east was a badly eroded and blocked room (Ab/Ac) which appeared to be L-shaped and led into a thin chamber with a north-south axis roughly 1.6m by 3.7m.

Off the southern end of the shaft was another large room (B), plastered but blackened with soot, which had niches down the side which appeared to lead to rooms at a lower level.

Figure 73. The western large shaft as found.

Straight ahead, to the south, was a second room (Bb) with two niches on each of its three sides (south, east and west, the entrance being to the north). Below that room separated by roughly 20cms of rock, was another room so choked with debris that it was possible to see only ten to fifteen centimetres of clearance between the debris filling it and the ceiling.

Figure 74. The shaft bottom looking north.   *Figure 75. the shaft bottom looking south.*

In all we were able to enter six rooms, with the possibility of a further five rooms existing mostly at lower levels. Photographic opportunities on this occasion were not perfect but there is a possibility that the first southern room entered was of double the height of the other rooms. The shaft size (3m by 1.5m) would have permitted the introduction of fairly large coffins. However, the bottom of the shaft was so filled with rubble that its ultimate profile and depth remain unclear.

Figure 76. The northern chamber (A) looking east.

Figure 77. The southern chamber (B) showing niches.

Figure 78. Room off main southern chamber (B) at lower level.

Figure 79. Main southern chamber (B) looking south to upper niched room. Lower room visible at right.

Figure 80. Niched chamber (Ba) directly to south of main southern chamber.

On the surface, scattered around the spoil-heaps there were, in addition to the pottery sherds, fragments of faience and tiny pieces of green stone from some worked object, possibly a stone vessel.

It is highly unlikely that Carter entered these tombs. Imposing the rough plan sketched on site afterwards onto a Google earth enlargement of the site makes it likely that the tomb we examined joins the large shaft to its north-east. It is possible that some of the apparent doors from chamber to chamber which we saw were robbers' holes and not part of the original architecture. The architecture of these tombs is, nonetheless, highly unusual and on this basis alone the site merits further examination. Of known royal shaft tombs only AN B, the controversial late XVIIth or early XVIIIth dynasty burial (thought by Carter to be that of Amenhotep I) has chambers on different levels.

In addition, there is a wealth of dateable material and the hope must remain that within these tombs there is some indication of the names and status of the people buried here.

The pottery appears to be D-ware common between the reigns of Amenhotep III and Ramesses II and this corroborates Carter's estimate of an Amenhotep III date.

Conclusions

The importance of this site for our mission is that it appears to confirm, subject to dating, that the burials of family members moved steadily westwards as the XVIIIth dynasty progressed. It certainly confirms that the extent of the Theban necropolis is far more extensive than is currently accepted. A north-westward expansion also makes it all the more acceptable that the original activity in Wadi F dates to the reigns of the XVIIIth dynasty kings whose names appear there.

Carter's article of 1917[31], and the work of many who have examined the evidence that article produced, has implicitly assumed that the move away from the Theban Massif into the Western Wadis was motivated by a search for hiding places for family members.

This apparently complex burial site could not be more exposed or more different from the clefts and ravines in which the burials of the Western Wadis are secreted. There is no possibility here of burials with female anatomical symbolism. The siting of these monuments seems almost reckless. Does this brazen disregard for security reflect the confidence of an imperial age which had yet to encounter the self-doubt and insecurity which may have resulted from the Amarna Period? Until this site is properly excavated it raises more questions than it answers.

---

[31] Carter, H. op. cit..

Figure 81. Pottery fragments.

Figure 82. The site from the south-west showing the size of the spoil-heaps.

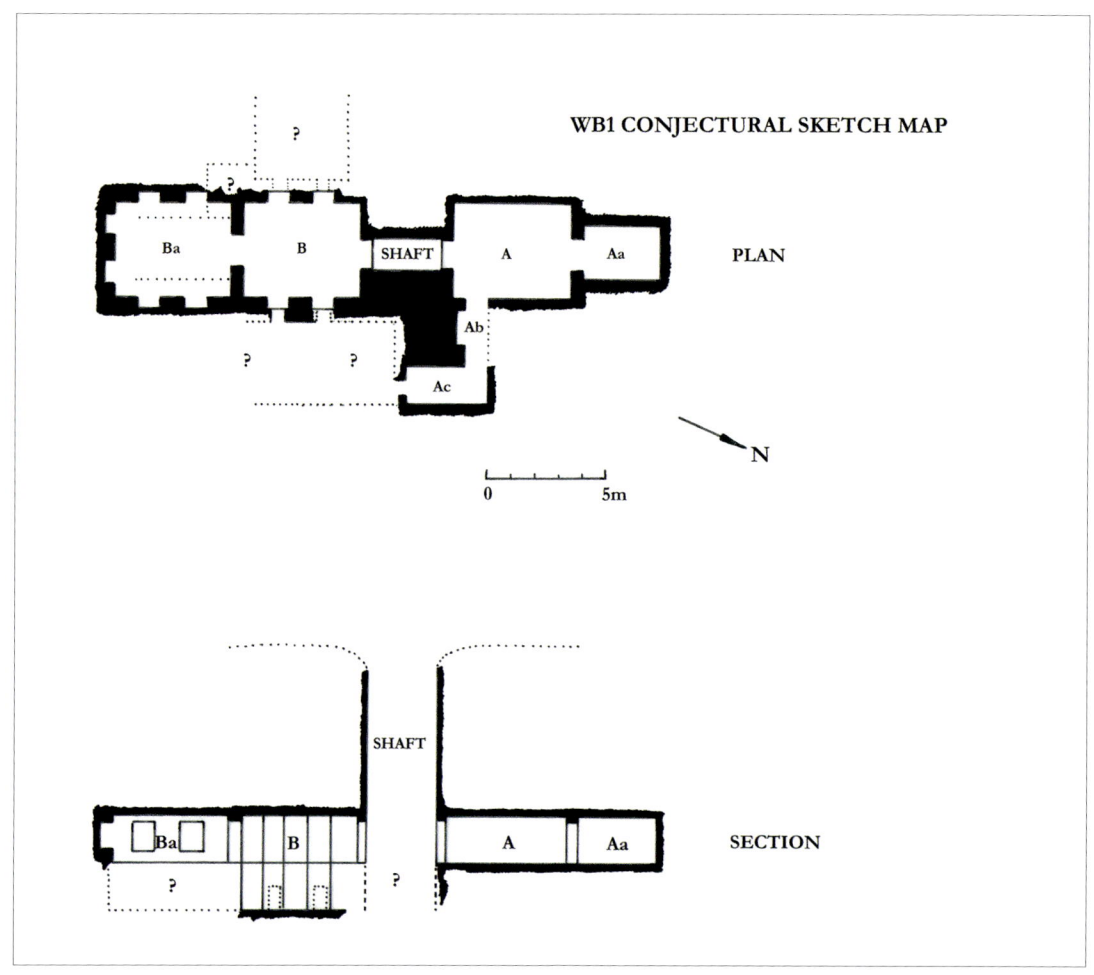

Figure 83. Conjectural sketch plan made on site after investigation of western large shaft. Only very roughly to scale and as rooms blocked with debris many features are inferred.

The Western Wadis of the Theban Necropolis

CHAPTER ELEVEN - The roads and pathways of the Theban Necropolis

One of the features which accompanies the location of tombs in these Western Wadis and, in turn, suggests the presence of burial activity in other, as yet unexplored, wadis still further afield, is the network of ancient paths which radiate east and west from the twin spines of the two ancient roads running northwards from the main Theban Massif *(Figure 84)*.

Figure 84. Some of the major pathways across the Theban hills.

Examining these on Google earth or satellite photographs is not without its problems. The two main ancient roads have often been re-used by modern traffic or, in the case of the eastern road, have been obliterated by modern vehicle traffic. Many of the lower tracks, especially those nearer the cultivation, have been created in modern times by local people searching for gypsum and fertiliser. Distinguishing ancient from modern is difficult. Some of the ancient roads shown clearly on early maps have also disappeared or, given the approximation of their positions in those early maps, are difficult to reconcile with modern aerial views.

Figure 85. The high desert road east of the Western Wadis.

Figure 86. Hut on the high desert road to the east of Wadi A.

Despite these observations, modern tracks made in search of gypsum and fertiliser generally end in pits of one sort or another and can be distinguished from a type of path of particular archaeological interest: the cliff-top path. The eastern side of the vast

Wadi El-Agala has paths which trace their routes along the tops of cliffs in such a way as cannot be explained by short-cuts or optimum walking routes. The same can be said of the eastern side of the northern part of the Wadi Bariya and the un-named wadis to the north of the West Valley of the Valley of the Kings. These cliff-top paths connect with the high desert road. Even with the best photographs, however, tracks seem to fade or end abruptly and paths which show up at ground level to inspection on foot, often cannot be seen when viewing from a higher level.

Cliff-top tracks suggest patrolling activity monitoring sites below. They are present above all the Western Wadis where there are tombs (A, C, and D). As Figure 5 shows, they run along cliff-tops far to the north and west of the Western Wadis.

The primary purpose of the high desert routes is not clear. However, once up on the high desert, travel is much faster than it is in the wadis below. Having struggled up to the high desert from Wadi F we were surprised by how quickly we were able to walk to the south-western point of the high desert above the 'Valley of the Queens'.

As mentioned above, we found no evidence in the high desert of water-storage or of water-gathering but as can be seen from Figure 55 we only followed a single route up out of Wadi F and back to Medinet Habu. There was some evidence of efflorescence in the cliffs indicative of the presence of moisture in the limestone layers but none near the wadi floors.

For workmen travelling from Deir el-Medina to these remoter sites, a route up to the saddle below El Qurn, westwards to the north and below that peak and then up onto the western high desert road *(Figure 84)* would most likely have been far quicker than a route along the wadi floors.

The length of time necessary to excavate tombs in the wadis is difficult to estimate. In Wadi F there is what might be a record of days. There is a rough underhang on which small vertical notches have been cut. The area has broken away in places so interpretation is almost impossible. These notches are not divided into ancient Egyptian weeks of eight days and so they may relate to something quite different. It would not, however, have taken much more than the seven modern weeks' worth of notches to cut a simple tomb so the scale of supplies for the workmen here would not have been enormous.

The path from the high desert down into Wadi F is, as has been observed, extremely steep. A man, or two men, carrying a water jar would have found the descent on the path we took perilous. There may have been better paths up onto the high desert but none was obvious to us *(Figures 52 and 55)*.

We did not inspect the more northerly route marked by Carter on his sketch map, nor did we inspect the area where the gulley descending from the high desert meets the cliff-tops.

It seems likely that these high desert routes were used for policing burial sites. Paths run all over the Theban hills to and from the larger settlement sites in the saddles between the Valley of the Kings and Deir el-Medina and on the small plateau to the south of Wadi A *(Figure 6)*. It is less clear whether they would have been used for supplying the temporary encampments of workmen excavating tombs. These encampments had to be supplied with food, water, chisels, lamp-oil and wicks. We found no evidence suggesting how this was done.

To the west of the two roads which run north from the main Theban Massif there is another road, mentioned by Carter in connection with the Wadi Bariya site. The southernmost point of this road is 200m south of the shaft-tombs of the WB1 site. It then runs northwards to the west of Wadi Bariya and joins the other two roads on the high desert after 7.5 kilometres *(Figure 5)*.

CHAPTER TWELVE - Conclusions

Carter's work in the Western Wadis brought together a number of elements: cliff-tombs and shaft-tombs of the XVIIIth dynasty; graffiti; paths and roads; settlements. His focus on the monuments of leading royal figures meant that the relationship between these elements was over-shadowed by his concentration on Hatshepsut's cliff-tomb and the sarcophagus prepared for that tomb.

It is clear from our re-examination of these wadis that there was burial activity in the XVIIIth dynasty over a much broader area than has been fully appreciated hitherto. This extended as far west as the WB1 site and may have included as yet unconfirmed activity in Wadis F and G.

The graffiti in these wadis appears to be of a number of types including:

a) prehistoric;

b) XVIIIth dynasty;

c) late XXth and early XXIst dynasty;

d) Coptic;

c) modern.

From what is known from the more extensive coverage of Wadis A, C and D and from the known activity of certain members of the Deir el-Medina workmen's village in clearing burials in the reigns of the High Priest Kings of Upper Egypt in the late XXth and early XXIst dynasties, it seems reasonable to assume that it was the XVIIIth dynasty that these wadis were used for interments.

Subsequently the wadis were seemingly examined by surveyors, masons and workmen over an indeterminate period contemporaneous with the apparently systematic clearances taking place in the other parts of the Theban Necropoleis in the late XXth and early XXIst dynasties. The principal evidence for this programme of clearance comes from the dockets recording the movements of the bodies found in the royal caches and recorded by Nicholas Reeves[32]. These mention names which recur in the graffiti present in the Western Wadis in and around the known and likely sites of earlier burials.

The roads and pathways of the Theban necropoleis form a more complex and more extensive network than has been appreciated. The precise role of the major "roads" which eventually seem to cut across the Qena Bend is unclear. The radiating trackways which descend into the various wadis to the cliff-tops of the Wadi El-Agala and the

---

[32] Reeves, C.N. 1990 'Valley of the Kings', KPI, London. pp244-5.

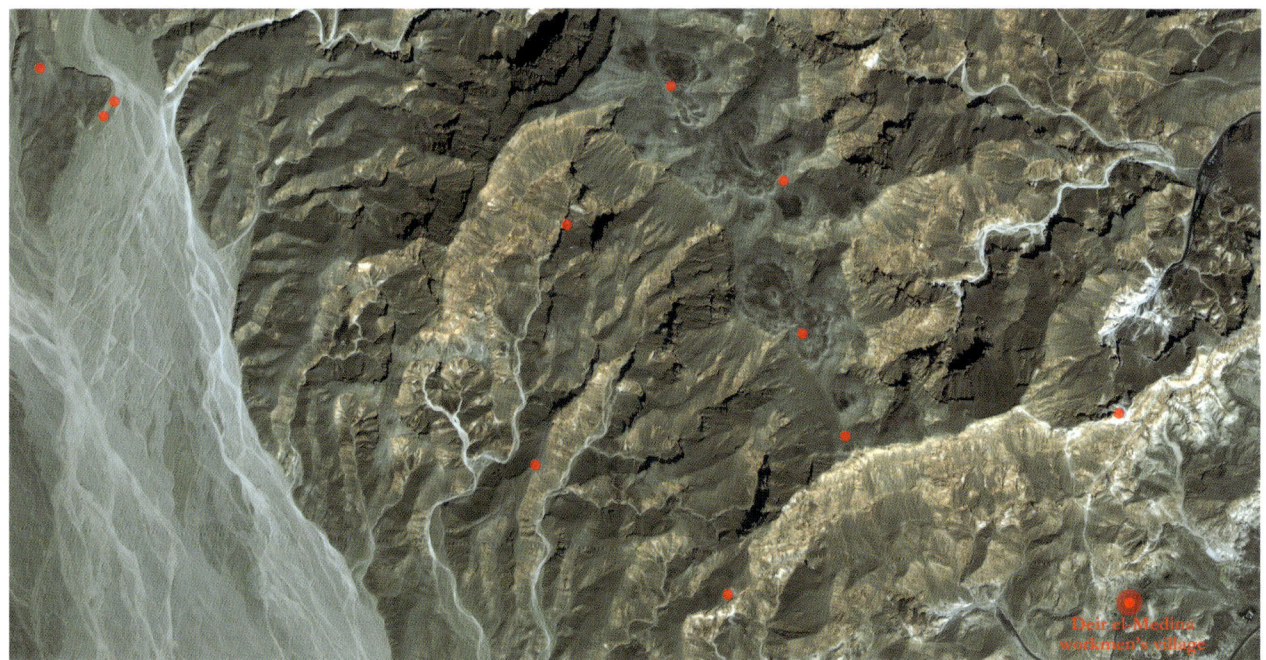

Figure 87. The known locations of workmen's huts. These exclude the large numbers of huts built in the Valley of the Kings main valley and in the West Valley.

north-eastern side of the Wadi Bariya. This suggests the likelihood that these areas were patrolled in ancient times and that, in turn, suggests the possibility that the burial grounds of the Theban necropoleis extended much, much further than has been understood.

Given the role of the 'Valley of the Queens' in providing a burial ground for the royal families of the XIXth and XXth dynasties, and the relatively small number of known burials of the XVIIIth dynasty royal family in the necropolis as a whole, a reasonable hypothesis would indicate that, if there are burials concealed in the cliffs in these more remote locations, they relate to the XVIIIth dynasty.

The surprisingly open nature of the burials in the WB1 site suggest that it is not only in the hidden clefts and gullies of these more distant locations that further investigation should focus.

The presence of settlements has often been noted but no study has so far connected the many sites where these occur and analysed their relationship (Figure 87). There were extensive settlements in the Wadi Bariya and at the top of the cliffs leading to Wadi A quite different in nature from the occasional huts encountered in wadis and on high ground. Further study of these would be helpful to a better understanding of the overall Theban necropoleis.

The Wadi F and Wadi G sites merit excavation. It is not unlikely that if burials were located there they would be on a similar scale to those in Wadis A, C and D. the likelihood is that the interments would be those of female members of the royal family.

If Carter's analysis of the date of the WB1 site is correct, as our preliminary pottery indications suggest, then there is already confirmation of burial activity to the west of the Western Wadis.

The complexity of the geology in Wadi F makes this a daunting site. Any confirmation or elimination of evidence of XVIIIth dynasty burial activity would be an extremely expensive enterprise. On the other hand, the 127 cleft in Wadi G and its related shaft-tombs on the "tongue" would be much simpler to investigate more thoroughly.

The WB1 site deserves investigation on account of the unusual architecture of the shaft-tombs alone. Its open position, its location at the end of a major road heading north into the high desert, the presence of numbers of huts both above and below the site and the illicit activity which has already resulted in the loss of a substantial amount of information are all additional reasons to re-clear these shaft tombs.

Should they provide confirmation of the westward and northward shift in the family burial ground during the XVIIIth dynasty, as seems likely, then they, and the road networks visible further north also point to the need for further exploration of the Wadi Bariya and Wadi El-Agala.

Piers Litherland
New Kingdom Research Foundation
May, 2014

APPENDICES

Select Bibliography

ARNOLD, D. 1991 "Building in Ancient Egypt". Oxford University Press, Oxford.

AUBRY, M. et al. 2008 (Aubry, M.-P.; Berggren, W., Dupuis, C.,Ghaly, H., Ward, D., King, C., Knox, R.;,Ouda, K., Youssef, M., Galal, W.) "Pharaonic Necrostratigraphy: A review of Geological and Archaeological Studies in the Theban Necroplis, Luxor, West Bank, Egypt" Terra Nova, 21 (4).

BASEL, University of: http://aegyptologie.unibas.ch/forschung/projekte/university-of-basel-kings-valley-project

BARAIZE, E. 1921 "Rapport sur la decouverte d'un tombeau de la XVIIIe dynastie a Sikket Taqet Zayed", Annales du Service des Antiquites d'Egypte 21, ASAE, Cairo.

BIERBRIER, M. 1989 The Tomb Builders of the Pharaohs. American University in Cairo Press.

BRYAN B. 2001 "Temples of Millions of Years" in Kent R. Weeks ed. "The Treasures of the Valley of the Kings: Tombs and Temples of the Theban West Bank in Luxor" American University in Cairo Press, Cairo.

BRYAN, B. 2000 "The Eighteenth Dynasty before the Amarna Period" Chapter 9 in Shaw, I. ed. Oxford History of Ancient Egypt, Oxford University Press, Oxford.

CARNARVON and **CARTER, H. 1912** "Five Years' Exploration at Thebes". Oxford University Press, Oxford.

CARTER, H. 1916 "Report of the tomb of Zeser-ka-re Amenhetep I". JEA 3.

CARTER, H. 1917 "A Tomb Prepared for Queen Hatshepsuit and other Recent Discoveries at Thebes", the Journal of Egyptian Archaeology, Volume 4, No 2/3 (April-July, 1917), Egypt Exploration Society, London.

ČERNÝ, J. 2001 "A Community of Workmen at Thebes in the Ramesside Period". Institut francais d'archéologie orientale, Le Caire.

ČERNÝ, J., and **SADEK, A.** 1971 "Graffiti de la montagne thébaine". Institut francais d'archéologie orientale, Le Caire.

CLINE, E. and **O'CONNOR, D., ed. 2006** "Thutmose III" The University of Michigan Press, Ann Arbor.

CROSS, S. 2008 The Hydrology of the Valley of the Kings. JEA 94.

CURTIS, G. 1995 "Deterioration of the Royal Tombs." in Wilkinson, R. (ed.), "Valley of the Sun Kings: New Expeditions in the Tombs of the Pharaohs". University of Arizona Egyptian Expedition, Tucson.

DODSON, A. 2009 "Amarna Sunset." The American University in Cairo Press, Cairo.

DODSON, A. 2000 "The Burial of the Royal Family during the Eighteenth Dynasty" in Hawass, Z. ed. "Egyptology at the Dawn of the Twenty-First Century: Proceedings of the Eighth International Congress of Egyptologists", American University in Cairo Press Cairo.

DODSON, A. and **HITTON, D.** 2004. "The Complete Royal Families of Ancient Egypt". Thames & Hudson, London.

DODSON, A. and **IKRAM, S. 2008** "The Tomb in Ancient Egypt". Thames & Hudson, London.

DORFMAN, P. and **BRYAN, B. 2007** "Sacred Space and Sacred Function in Ancient Thebes". Oriental Institute of the University of Chicago, Chicago.

DZIOBEK, E., HOVELER-MILLER, M. and **LOEBEN, C. ed. 2009** "The Mysterious Tomb 63: The latest discovery in the Valley of the Kings". Verlag Marie Leidorf GmbH, Rahden.

GRAEFE, E. and **BELOVA, G. 2010** "The Royal Cache TT320". SCA Press, Cairo.

HAENY, G. 1998 "New Kingdom 'Mortuary Temples' and 'Mansions of Millions of Years'" in Shafer, B. ed. 1998 "Temples of Ancient Egypt". I.B. Tauris, London.

HARRIS, J. and **WENTE, E.** 1980 ed. "An X-Ray Atlas of the Royal Mummies". University of Chicago Press, Chicago.

HAWASS, Z. 2009 "The Lost Tombs of Thebes". Thames & Hudson. London.

HAYES, W. 1935 "Sarcophagi of the XVIIIth Dynasty". University Press, Princeton.

HORNUNG, E. 1990 "Valley of the Kings – Horizon of Eternity". Timken Publishers, New York.

HORNUNG, E. 2001A "Funerary Literature in the Tombs of Valley of the Kings"" in Kent R. Weeks ed. "The Treasures of the Valley of the Kings: Tombs and Temples of the Theban West Bank in Luxor" American University in Cairo Press, Cairo.

HOVING, T. 1978 "Tutankhamun: The Untold Story". Hamish Hamilton, London.

JAMES, T. 1992 Howard Carter: The Path to Tutankhamun. Kegan Paul International, London.

JAMES, T. 2001 "The Tomb of Horemheb" in Weeks, K. ed. "The Treasures of the Valley of the Kings: Tombs and Temples of the Theban West Bank in Luxor" American University in Cairo Press, Cairo.

JANOT, F. 2008 "The Royal Mummies" American University in Cairo Press, Cairo.

KLEMM, R. and **KLEMM, D.** 2008 "Stones and Quarries In Ancient Egypt". British Musuem Press, London.

LEBLANC, C. 1989 "Ta Set Neferou", Nubar Publishing House, Cairo.

LILYQUIST, C. 2003 "The Tomb of the Three Foreign Wives of Tutmose III". Metropolitan Museum of Art, New York.

PEDEN, A. 2001 "The Graffiti of Pharaonic Egypt", Brill, Leiden, Boston, Cologne.

PIANKOFF, A. 1955 "The Shrines of Tut-Ankh-Amon" Pantheon Books, New York.

PORTER, B. and **MOSS, R.** 1964 Topographical Bibliography of Ancient Egyptian Hieroglyphic Texts, Reliefs, and Paintings I: The Theban Necropolis, Part 2, Royal Tombs and Smaller Cemeteries. Clarendon Press. Oxford.

QUIRKE, S. 1991 "The Cult of Ra". Thames & Hudson, London.

QUIRKE, S. 1996 "Hieroglyphs and the Afterlife". British Museum Press, London.

QUIRKE, S. ed. 1997 "The Temple in Ancient Egypt". British Museum Press, London

REEVES, C.N. 1990 "Valley of the Kings: The Decline of a Royal Necropolis". Studies in Egyptology. Kegan Paul International, London.

REEVES, C.N., ed. "After Tutankhamun: Research and Excavation in the Royal Necropolis at Thebes". KPI, London.

REEVES, C.N. and **WILKINSON, R.** 1996 "The Complete Valley of the Kings". Thames and Hudson, London.

ROMER, J. 1984 "Ancient Lives". Michael O'Mara Books, London.

ROMER, J. 1981 "Valley of the Kings". Michael Joseph, London.

RUTHERFORD, J. "Tentative Tomb Protection Priorities, Valley of the Kings, Egypt." in Wilkinson, R. (ed.), "Valley of the Sun Kings: New Expeditions in the Tombs of the Pharaohs". University of Arizona Egyptian Expedition, Tucson.

RYAN, D. 1992 "Some Observations Concerning Uninscribed Tombs in the Valley of the Kings" in Reeves, C.N., ed. "After Tutankhamun: Research and Excavation in the Royal Necropolis at Thebes". KPI, London.

RYAN, D. 2010 "Beneath the Sand of Egypt". Harper Collins, New York.

RYAN, D. "Further Observations Concerning the Valley of the Kings." in Wilkinson, R. (ed.), "Valley of the Sun Kings: New Expeditions in the Tombs of the Pharaohs". University of Arizona Egyptian Expedition, Tucson.

RZEPKA, S. 2000 "Rock graffiti above the temple of Hatshepsut", Polish Archaeology in the Mediterranean XI, Warsaw.

SHAFER, B. ed. **1998** "Temples of Ancient Egypt". I.B. Tauris, London.

SHAW, I. 2003 Exploring Ancient Egypt. Oxford University Press, Oxford.

STRUDWICK, N. & H. 1999 Thebes in Egypt. British Museum Press, London.

STRUDWICK, N. and **TAYLOR, J. 2003** "The Theban Necropolis" British Museum Press, London.

THOMAS, E. 1966 The Royal Necropoleis of Thebes. Princeton: privately printed.

VANDERSLAYEN, C. 1995 "Who was the First King in the Valley of the Kings?" in Wilkinson, R. (ed.), "Valley of the Sun Kings: New Expeditions in the Tombs of the Pharaohs". University of Arizona Egyptian Expedition, Tucson.

WEEKS, K. 2001 ed. "The Treasures of the Valley of the Kings: Tombs and Temples of the Theban West Bank in Luxor" American University in Cairo Press, Cairo.

WEEKS, K. et al. 2006 Valley of the Kings Site Management Masterplan. Theban Mapping Project Publication, Cairo.

WEEKS, K. 1995 "The Work of the Theban Mapping Project and the Protection of the Valley of the Kings." in Wilkinson, R. (ed.), "Valley of the Sun Kings: New Expeditions in the Tombs of the Pharaohs". University of Arizona Egyptian Expedition, Tucson.

WEEKS, K. 1998 "The Lost Tomb". William Morrow and Company, New York.

WEEKS, K., ed. 2000 Atlas of the Valley of the Kings. Publications of the Theban Mapping Project, American University in Cairo Press, Cairo.

WILKINSON, R. 1994 "Symbolic Location and Alignment in New Kingdom Royal Tombs and Their Decoration." Journal of the American Research Center in Egypt 31.

WILKINSON, R. 2003 "The Complete Gods & Goddesses of Ancient Egypt". Thames & Hudson, London.

WILKINSON, R. 2000 "The Complete Temples of Ancient Egypt". Thames & Hudson, London.

WINLOCK, H. 1924 "The Tombs of the Kings of the Seventeenth Dynasty at Thebes". Journal of Egyptian Archaeology 10.Picture credits

Picture Credits

Figure 1   Carter, H. 1917 "A Tomb Prepared for Queen Hatshepsuit and other Recent Discoveries at Thebes", the Journal of Egyptian Archaeology, Volume 4, No 2/3 (April-July, 1917), Egypt Exploration Society, London. Plate XIX.

Figure 2   Griffith Institute, University of Oxford, Carter MSS.

Figure 3   Mapmart.

Figure 4   Mapmart.

Figure 5   Mapmart.

Figure 6   Mapmart.

Figure 7   Griffith Institute, University of Oxford, Carter MSS and JEA, 1917.

Figure 16   Apollo Mapping.

Figure 21   Griffith Institute, University of Oxford, Carter MSS.

Figure 22   Griffith Institute, University of Oxford, Carter MSS and NKRF.

Figure 23   Griffith Institute, University of Oxford, Carter MSS and NKRF.

Figure 26   Griffith Institute, University of Oxford, Carter MSS and JEA, 1917.

Figure 28   Apollo Mapping.

Figure 33   Adapted from Lilyquist, The Three Foreign Wives of Thutmose III.

Figure 37   Griffith Institute, University of Oxford, Carter MSS and JEA, 1917.

Figure 38   Mapmart.

Figure 40   Mapmart.

Figure 47   Griffith Institute, University of Oxford, Carter MSS and JEA, 1917.

Figure 55   Apollo Mapping.

Figure 56   Mapmart.

Figure 57   Apollo Mapping and Griffith Institute, University of Oxford, Carter MSS.

Figure 58   Apollo Mapping and JEA, 1917.

Figure 66   JEA, 1917.

Figure 67   Adapted from Google Earth.

Figure 84   Mapmart.

All other photographs and diagrams were taken by, or produced by, the New Kingdom Research Foundation team and are copyright.

INDEX

Akhetaten 14

Amenhotep II 10, 11, 44, 56, 57

Amenhotep III 10, 11

Ankhefenamun 36

Baraize, E 11, 22, 23, 26, 29, 30, 45

Bunbury, Judith 19, 27

Butehamun 23, 26, 27, 36, 37, 42, 43, 57, 58

Carnarvon, Lord 10, 11

Carter, Howard 10, 11, 13, 22, 24, 26, 27, 30, 34, 35, 36, 37, 40, 42, 47, 48, 52, 53, 54, 55, 56, 58, 59, 60, 61, 64, 65, 67, 68, 70, 71, 72, 73, 80, 86, 87, 89

Černy, Jaroslav 20, 23, 26, 36, 56

Dikhonsuiry 42, 67

Djehutymose 36, 57

Goddard, Stephen 19

Griffith Institute 9, 11, 36, 39, 47, 65

Hanan Hassan Ahmed Hussein 19, 36, 73

Hatshepsut 10, 11, 21, 23, 24, 26, 28, 30, 45, 87

Herihor 26, 41, 58-9

Kamel, Mohsen 19

LeBlanc, C 18

Lilyquist, Christine 11, 36, 41, 43, 58

Martin, Geoffrey 19, 37

Mehafto 36

Montuseankh 57

Nainudjem or Nau-nedjem 23, 36

Nefrure 11, 35, 36, 37

Peden, A 56, 58

Pinudjem I 26

Pinudjem II 26

Reeves, C N 26, 58, 87

Romer, J 58

Rzefka, S 23

Smendes 26

Smith, Graham 19

Thomas, Elizabeth 11, 22, 23, 35, 36, 64, 71

Thutmose II 11

Thutmose III 11, 43, 44, 56

Ti'aa 10

Tomb 20 22, 30

Tomb 21 22, 30

Tomb 22 22, 30

Tomb 23 22, 30

Tomb 29 22, 30

Tomb AN B 18

Tomb KV20 18

Tomb KV21 10

Tomb KV32 10

Tomb KV34 18

Tomb KV35 10, 44

Tomb KV38 18

Tomb KV39 18

Tomb KV40 10

Tomb KV43 18

Tomb KV60 10

Tomb WV22 10

Wadi A 21-33

Wadi B 71-72

Wadi Bariya 18

Wadi Bariya Site (WB 1) 73-82, 88

Wadi C 34-40

Wadi D 41-47

Wadi E 72

Wadi El-Gharbi 17-18

Wadi F 48-63

Wadi G 64-70

Wadi Gabbanat El-Qurud 17

Piers Litherland was born in Central Africa, was educated in Britain and worked for many years in Asia. He received his undergraduate degree from Oxford University and an M. Phil in Egyptology from Cambridge University. He is a director of Ancient Egyptian Research Associates (A.E.R.A.) and of the New Kingdom Research Foundation.